THE
GOOD
THE
BAD
& THE
RUGBY

RELOADED

THE
GOOD
THE
BAD
& THE
RUGBY

RELOADED

THIS TIME IT'S PERSONAL

ALEX PAYNE   **JAMES HASKELL**   **MIKE TINDALL**

HarperCollins*Publishers*

HarperCollins*Publishers*
1 London Bridge Street
London SE1 9GF

www.harpercollins.co.uk

HarperCollins*Publishers*
Macken House, 39/40 Mayor Street Upper
Dublin 1, D01 C9W8, Ireland

First published by HarperCollins*Publishers* 2025

1 3 5 7 9 10 8 6 4 2

HB ISBN 978-0-00-878637-3
Signed edition ISBN 978-0-00-879852-9

Printed and bound in the UK using 100%
renewable electricity at CPI Group (UK) Ltd

MIX
Paper | Supporting
responsible forestry
FSC
www.fsc.org
FSC™ C007454

This book contains FSC™ certified paper and other controlled
sources to ensure responsible forest management.

For more information visit: www.harpercollins.co.uk/green

Payno: To my wife, my girl and my boy.
My world.

Hask: To my daughter Bodhi, my greatest inspiration.
To Dad, who always believed in me, pushed me to do
right by rugby and was one of my biggest fans, thank you.
And to my mum, who somehow manages to turn up
at every event, ticket or no ticket. Your support
never goes unnoticed.

Tins: To our fans. All eight of you.
Thank you for getting it. Whatever 'it' is.

CONTENTS

Introduction   1

1. You'll never make any money   3
2. An itch that needed scratching   13
3. I knew how much he loved me   25
4. I'm young, I'm keen, I'll do anything   61
5. Not very fast, can't pass, can't kick   73
6. *FishOMania*   83
7. Amazed to be playing rugby   93
8. I might become a broadcaster   103
9. Unbreakable   111
10. Don't fuck it up, mate   125
11. A word from our sponsor   139
12. Quite a funny bunch   149
13. The greatest female darts player of all time?   161
14. Jekyll and Hydes   171
15. Brain fart   177
16. Stretchered off at Twickenham   193
17. Turning 40   203
18. A bit more dignified?   229

19. I thought I might punch someone 239

20. Smile because it happened 245

21. Inject it and strap it 257

22. Geech's funny turn 263

23. I've no idea who this bloke is 273

24. Not a rebel league 283

25. A sleeping giant 293

The thank yous 303

INTRODUCTION

PAYNO

As was widely predicted, our first book, *The Good, The Bad & The Rugby – Unleashed*, did not win a Pulitzer Prize. It did, however, scoop Sports Entertainment Book of the Year at the 2025 Charles Tyrwhitt Sports Book Awards (and sold quite a lot of copies), so here we are again, back for a sequel.

Much like Bob Dylan when he won the Nobel Prize in Literature, or the Academy Awards-shy Katherine Hepburn, none of us was able to attend the Sports Book Awards at The Oval cricket ground. When our nomination was announced, Hask texted to say, 'Prizes are nothing. My prize is my work'; and while Tins did appear via a pre-recorded telecast, I'm told that most attendees were shocked that he knew of the book's existence. As for me, I was probably busy trying to extinguish yet another podcast-related inferno started by Hask.

What more have we to say? It's a fair question. Hask has told his best stories so many times that this book is more likely to be nominated for a fiction award than a non-fiction one (as Tins often points out, stories that started out almost as throwaway lines can now last for up to half an hour, what with all the bells and whistles Hask has attached to them over the years).

Then again, Hask can mine more new material from a trip to the supermarket than most people can from an entire lifetime – and you won't be surprised to learn that he hasn't just been hanging around Waitrose since our last book came out. He recently turned 40, he's been through much personal turmoil, he's done an awful lot of DJing – and he's had a lot of arguments. Expect much of that, and even some thoughts on rugby, in the following pages.

When it comes to Tins, you'll find out about his early days in rugby, how he had to fight to make it, some of his highest highs and lowest lows, what he thinks of the state of the game, and his plans to get it back on track. Meanwhile, I'll tell you all about my career in broadcasting, from making ('disgusting') tea and coffee, and presenting some of the greatest rugby matches in history, to getting binned by Sky, and ending up on a podcast with one of English rugby's biggest legends and a member of the royal family. And Hask.

I should end by begging you to pardon my previous flippancy. It was, of course, lovely to win that award, as well as very surprising. In fact, *The Good, The Bad & The Rugby* will never stop surprising us, and its continuing success is largely down to you – our wonderful listeners, viewers, and now readers. We do hope you enjoy what follows and that you keep coming back for more.

1

YOU'LL NEVER MAKE ANY MONEY

TINS

My first memory of playing rugby would be inter-house games at Queen Elizabeth Grammar School (QEGS) in Wakefield. I was in Savile House (Thomas Savile being one of the school's founders), and being one of the bigger kids – and because kids' rugby was full contact in those days – I very much enjoyed the freedom of running through and over the top of defenders.

My dad had captained Otley, who were quite a big rugby club back in the day, but I never saw him play because he suffered a bad injury when he was 27. However, he made sure to tell me how good he was. A lot. And it was very apparent that he loved the game so much, as did most of his brothers and my granddad, all of whom played for Otley.

When I think of Otley the place, I think of freedom. My grandma lived there, so I'd wander from her house to the ground. I spent a lot of time in the clubhouse and have vivid memories of men in blazers drinking beer from tankards, although it would sometimes be difficult to see them through the cigarette smoke. And while my mum and dad were having a drink and a chat, we'd be running all over the place – the pitch, the stand (which wasn't exactly the Kop but seemed like it to an eight-year-old), and the steaming changing rooms with those old communal bathtubs – and enjoying every minute of it.

I loved playing back-row and didn't think I'd ever play anywhere else. However, when I was 14 a talented number eight called Tom Hird joined QEGS from a school in Doncaster, and my coach suggested I start playing centre instead. I wasn't having that. The way I saw it, this new kid should move, not me. But John managed to convince me to play one game there and I soon realised how easy it was to play in the backs compared to in the forwards. I was big for a centre, and quite fast, so particularly enjoyed one-on-ones.

I was one of those lads who needed to be outside, not stuck behind a desk staring at a book, and I wasn't great academically anyway, however hard I tried. I wasn't a big watcher of rugby either (there wasn't much on the TV back then, outside the Six Nations and World Cups there was only *Rugby Special* on Sundays). I wanted to be doing it, not standing on the sidelines or in front of the TV with itchy feet. Even now, I always have to be doing something. Thankfully, we didn't have mobile phones when I was a kid, and I had sport as a release, so I didn't have to worry about that.

Rugby was my first love, but I played lots of other sports. I was never really interested in hockey because the season clashed with rugby, and I soon got bored with cricket (I did get sucked back in during sixth form, when I realised you could have a couple of beers on the boundary). I was decent at athletics – hurdles, discus, shot putt, whatever they put me in for really – and I got quite far with high jump. I recently had an argument with an Aussie mate who claimed he jumped higher than me, and later that day he sent me his school records to prove it: his best was 2.03 metres, mine was 1.93 metres, so I conceded he was king but loved the fact he had obviously been called out on this before and knew exactly where the evidence was! But I was good enough to compete at the North of England trials, and high jump translated well to my rugby career: when Dave Alred brought in Aussie Rules-type jumping to catch balls and the cross-field contestable kick got its first outing, I still had that spring, at least off one leg.

School rugby games took place on Saturdays, and because I didn't want to give up my entire weekend, and I played so much rugby at school anyway, I never joined a club. Weirdly, given the amount of time I spent there, I never played for Otley, and while I trained at Sandal Rugby Club, I don't remember playing for them. Wakefield Rugby Club still existed back then, and our rugby master Trevor Barker had played for them, but I never turned out for them either. That's why I always say that my first actual club was Bath.

My dad was like me, in that he'd quite happily spend hours passing or kicking a ball in the garden, usually until Mum told him he had to do something else. And because injury had cut him down in his prime, I always felt he harboured a lot of unrealised dreams. He'd played against Headingley, who had Scotland's Ian McGeechan and

England's John Spencer in the centres, and he thought he was better than Spencer. Maybe he was, maybe he wasn't, but first he broke his leg (and got married in a full leg cast) and then he destroyed his ACL, before they knew about ACL injuries so they just removed his cartilage, which probably made it worse. His England dream over, maybe he lived out those dreams through me and my brother Ian.

I wouldn't say my dad was hard on me, but he was very honest. He had a habit of telling me everything I'd done wrong first, then telling me what I'd done well. It was always a fair appraisal of my performance, and it rubbed off on me. Instead of walking off the pitch thinking about the good stuff I'd done – even if I'd scored a hatful – I'd be thinking, *What could I have done better? Was I in the wrong position for that tackle? Should I have passed when I made that break?* It kept me grounded, ensured I never got carried away with myself and was always striving to get better.

But as long as I gave it my all, Dad would be happy. His attitude was, if you try, you can't be wrong, and you can work on the other stuff; but if you don't try, you're pretty much screwed. That's what I'll be like with my kids.

Dad would commentate while watching me play, but because he'd always stand behind the posts, so that he could better see space and running lines, he didn't bother anyone – apart from his sons. I'll never forget the time he stormed into the house and said to my mum, 'I've had it with that kid', before storming off again. When Ian turned up, I said to him, 'What have you done?', to which he replied, 'Dad was gobbing off behind the posts and I told him to fuck off.' I made a mental note never to make the same mistake, but fast forward five or six years, I was playing for the first XV, Dad was gobbing off behind the posts (he would probably say constructive ideas from someone who had been there and done it!), and I shouted, 'Can you just shut the fuck up?' He wasn't particularly happy about that either and it was the last time I said it.

Ian was a good player but suffered a knee injury while he was still at school and never really got back into it, which was a shame as I remember he was pretty skilful. That pretty much ended his rugby career, even though he did have a couple of run-outs later down the road. As for me, I captained Yorkshire and had a trial for the North of England when I was 16, but my journey was nothing like Hask's, who played for all the England age groups and was earmarked for big things before he'd even left school. Two years later, I had another trial for the North of England, and they put me at full-back. Apart from my future best mate, Bath and England team-mate Iain Balshaw dummying and skinning me, I thought I played pretty well, but I didn't get picked again.

Schoolboy rugby has always been cliquey, especially in those days. Too much about what school you went to, and I just don't think my face fitted very well. Luckily for me, the England Schoolboys coach was a guy called Geoff Wappett – he also was coach of Bradford Grammar School, who at the time were QEGS's big rivals. He liked the physical side of my game and he invited me to train with the North of England.

Alex Sanderson, this big bronze Adonis from Kirkham Grammar School, was the number eight, and we quickly became the best of battle buddies. Because I was still an outsider, I was slightly obsessed with smashing people, to make a point, but Alex was my main target. Every time he got the ball, I'd try to bury him, and vice versa. We were constantly at war on the training ground, but firm friends off it, and Geoff liked that kind of attitude. I think he also realised that while I wasn't the most naturally talented centre, I did things other centres didn't. Because I was a converted back-row, I'd always be over the ball, trying to steal it – what they call jackaling nowadays – and that wasn't really done by centres back then.

Geoff then got me a game for the South West against the Midlands, I played quite well, scored a couple of tries, and got an England Schools trial off the back of it. A bad first ten minutes must have counted against me, because I didn't get picked again, but Geoff, who was a fan of my physicality, told me to stick around and I ended up in the squad for the first game against France in the Five Nations (as it was back then) at Twickenham. I came on in the second half on the wing and wanted to make an impression. We put a high ball on their small winger and it gave me the chance I needed. Their winger went up for the ball and I managed to time my tackle perfectly, smashing him when he landed, which was a bit of a statement. Future Newcastle, Toulon and Northampton centre Tom May started ahead of me against France, but, in a peculiar twist, he then went on study leave for two weeks. I started two games in his place, and he never got back in.

Rugby had only just gone pro, and academies weren't really a thing back then. On top of that, my mum had told me that I'd never make any money from rugby and was very keen for me to go to university, so I still wasn't thinking about a rugby career. Even when I went on an England Schoolboys tour to Australia in 1997, I didn't think it would lead anywhere, despite it being an insanely good team, including Jonny Wilkinson, Andrew Sheridan, Iain Balshaw, David Flatman, Lee Mears, Steve Borthwick and Alex Sanderson.

However, while I was in Australia, a guy called Alan Martinovic, who coached Colston's School in Bristol (who'd beaten my QEGS team in the Daily Mail Cup final two years in a row) got in touch to say that Bath, who he was also involved with, might want to sign me. Only then did I think that I might play rugby for a living. Gloucester and Newcastle also showed an interest, and I remember phoning my mum up and saying, 'You know you said I'd never make any money from rugby? Well, I've got three offers …'

I went and looked at all three clubs, but while Gloucester and Newcastle wanted me to go to university, and I'd been accepted on a sports psychology course at Durham, Bath said they wanted me to join them immediately, give it my all for a year, and see where I got to. A few lads from the England Schoolboys tour were going there, including Balsh and Mearsy, so I deferred my degree, got a house with those two, and my journey as a proper rugby player began.

2

AN ITCH
THAT NEEDED
SCRATCHING

PAYNO

I'll never forget the first game of rugby I played, even though it was an inglorious beginning. I was eight, started on the bench, skipped on in the second half, stood out on the wing without touching the ball until the final whistle, then skipped off again. My parents were there on the touchline, although I don't remember what they said to me afterwards. Not a lot, probably.

I had an incredibly happy childhood, but like everyone I had various things to work through as a young kid, not least losing a sister, Laura, when I was six. You have no idea how these things affect you at the time but I'm sure they did, particularly around my confidence. But sport was definitely a solution. I soon put my flouncing debut behind me and went from not really enjoying rugby to absolutely loving it, as if somebody had flipped a switch in my head. No way am I comparing myself to Hask or Tins – I'm talking about a little prep school called Sandroyd in Wiltshire – but I was a half-decent player in that environment, mainly because I was quite brave and liked getting stuck in. And when people are telling you you're doing well at something, your confidence is sure to grow.

I'd do rugby summer camps in the holidays, to get fit for the new season, and our rugby master, Mr Fowler, made me captain in my final year. He was the first person to see something in me and no doubt ignited what spark was there. For the first time in my life I thought, *OK, I'm actually good at something*, and being recognised in that way didn't just boost my confidence on the rugby field, it made me feel more comfortable in other areas. My determination grew, my belief grew and it made me comfortable with aiming for Eton and beyond. My brother, who was a much better player than me, captained the team a few years later, and he'd probably say something similar.

Even at nine or ten, I'd get unbelievably nervous before games, which is ridiculous looking back on it, but I remember how much it meant. Despite it being almost 40 years ago, I can still remember playing my part in little old Sandroyd's first ever win over its greatest rivals, the mighty Port Regis (Mrs Tindall's alma mater, weirdly). It was on their turf, it was pouring with rain, Tom Hooper and Harry Balston scored our tries (back when a try was worth four points) and we won 8–0. It was such a big event that the whole school came out to clap us in when we returned on the mini-bus, and our celebration was to push Mr Fowler into the swimming pool, fully clothed. I caught up with an old team-mate from that day during the recent Lions tour and I brought it up. He had exactly the same memories, and added that he missed both conversions. So it's not just me.

Hask and Tins obviously tell far more glorious rugby tales, but everyone has their own moments, and I do think rugby is a game that gives you something above and beyond other team sports.

At 13, I was picked for and captained a team called Wessex, which was the best of the South West's smaller prep schools. Think of it as the British & Irish Lions for boys in a small pocket of England. But it meant a lot, and we'd play against all the big public schools in that area, such as Sherborne, Canford and Bryanston. When I got to Eton I made the A's in my first term, but the following year I very nearly cut off a finger on a bandsaw in an Art class. I can hear Hask and Tins snigger, but I missed the entire season and by the following year the team had moved on, I hadn't grown and it all rather fell away. So I was an enthusiastic but decidedly average player.

Back then, schools rugby wasn't very scientific. If you were big and/or quick, you were picked for the team; if you were neither big nor quick, however gutsy you might have been, you struggled to get a look in. There was very little in the way of conditioning or working on skills, it was a case of two practice sessions a week and a game at the weekend.

Compare that to schools rugby today: Hask and I have attended a couple of Continental Tyres Schools Cup finals at Twickenham and it is like watching professional outfits, with players so big they block out the sun and skills that are off the charts. That's because they're in the gym at 6 a.m. every morning, training for two hours every evening, and they're often coached by ex-internationals. Last year, two of the Harrow team signed professional contracts with Bath the day after the final. That's how small the gap is now.

I watched an extraordinary amount of sport, and particularly rugby, as a kid. I was a devotee of *Grandstand* and my first broadcasting heroes were *Rugby Special* presenters Chris Rea (the former Scotland international, not the singer-songwriter from Middlesbrough, though I do have a soft spot for 'Driving Home For Christmas') and his successor John Inverdale, as well as commentator Nigel Starmer-Smith. I'd watch the Five Nations obsessively and got into trouble at school for sneaking into staff rooms and watching games during the 1995 World Cup in South Africa.

I'd get a rugby video every birthday, and I distinctly remember watching *Bill's Best Bits* (with the great Bill McLaren) for about the 250th time and my mum walking in and saying, 'For heaven's sake, you've got to get yourself motivated to do other things because you'll never have a job watching rugby …' I don't often remind her of that, but I do slip it into conversation when the need arises.

Like a lot of sports broadcasters, I was a frustrated schoolboy sportsman, who instinctively understood that while I loved the game, I was never going to achieve anything as a player. But I didn't just love the action on the field, I also loved the background stories and the people involved in the sport, at all levels. That being the case, I probably should have studied something to do with journalism at university, instead of history of art.

Before starting at Edinburgh University, I was a wannabe Jack Kerouac and drove around America for six months in an *A-Team* van with three friends, which was a proper adventure. I ended up playing in a sevens tournament in Dallas where at the afterparty, the captain of one of the other teams put one of his debutants through his initiation, which made my eyes water. He made the new recruit sink a beer and then headbutted him square in the face, breaking his nose. This bloke just accepted it but – can I surprise you? – that side of rugby was never really my thing.

I went for trials at university, but quickly realised that kind of rugby set-up didn't really float my boat. I get the rugby scene, and I completely understand for some it is their natural habitat, and good luck to them. Everyone needs their outlet. Hask and Tins are always telling me I'm a sipper and tipper, but the truth is I know what I like and I like what I know. When it comes to a night out, I like to play to my own rules rather than someone else's, because there's no point taking a driver off the tee when you know you're going to perform better by playing it safe with a four iron. I'm someone who wants to make the most of the whole night and to be there at the end, not carried out on a stretcher by 7 p.m.

It's a lesson I learned from my dad when I was about 16. We were on a skiing holiday once and our rep, some 18-year-old ski bum, was desperately trying to get him to drink shots at the bar. I was pushing him to show what he could do: 'Go on, Dad, you've got to drink them.' He put down his whisky, smiled and said to both of us, 'No, really, I'm OK, thanks.' I felt quite embarrassed and mildly let down, but my uncle took me aside and said, 'There will come a point in time when you realise that your old man is absolutely right – he's got nothing to prove to you. And he definitely has nothing to prove to the rep.'

A number of years later the penny dropped. Hask and Tins will tell you that I'm incredibly stubborn in that regard. I plough my own furrow, instead of doing things other people might want me to do, and no man was going to make me drink a pint of vomit at Edinburgh, mine or anyone else's.

I ended up playing a fair amount of wonderfully average rugby over my four years in Edinburgh. There was a vibrant inter-mural rugby scene every Wednesday, involving 20 teams playing a full league season. We actually had a pretty good side, losing in the final in our penultimate year and winning the competition in my final year. There were some fantastic teams and players in the competition, including future Scotland scrum-half Rory Lawson, who has become a good mate after we worked together for years at Sky, and his brother and future Scotland sevens star Gregor. I also played sevens against Simon Taylor, not long before he was picked for Scotland and then the Lions. As you can imagine, he was extraordinarily good.

At the weekends I also played for Edinburgh Academicals; the oldest surviving football club of any code in Scotland, having been formed in 1857. Accies have produced countless Scotland internationals and nine British & Irish Lions, and while I never reached such heights with the club, I was part of a pretty good Under-21s squad. And while I only played a few games for the firsts, I went as far as I was ever going to, which is all you can really ask.

I was a pretty skinny student, fit and fairly brave, but certainly not tough. I remember going to training with the firsts one Thursday, and it was essentially a brawl in the mud. I hung on in there, was put on the bench for a cup game on the Saturday, came on and did very little in a game we should never have lost. I remember the coach tearing an absolute strip off us in the changing room afterwards and saying that anyone who wasn't at training on Tuesday wouldn't play again that season. Needless to say I didn't make training, dropped back to the Under-21s and that was that.

We did have some great trips, though, the highlight being the evening before every Scotland v England match in the Six Nations, when Accies would play London Scottish in the same city as the Calcutta Cup was being contested. On one trip down south for the fixture, the plan was to catch the 9 a.m. train from Edinburgh, be in London for 1 p.m., have a bit of lunch before stretching the legs, then be at Richmond Athletic Ground for a 7.45 kick-off. Unfortunately, all trains out of Edinburgh were cancelled because of snow, so we ended up taking a bus, arriving at the ground at 7.30, changing, running out and getting licked by 50 points. They had a couple of centres who'd played Super Rugby, and I don't think we got a hand on them all night.

Accies was packed with great people, though, and I actually took Hask and Tins back a few years ago to do a show in their new clubhouse. It turned into one of those nights; in the small hours we found ourselves deep in an Edinburgh dungeon sipping some of the finest whisky on earth. As you do.

As much as I loved playing and was thankful for the good times it had given me, I can't pretend to have been anything other than a decidedly average player. So when I left Edinburgh, I didn't think, *Cool, I had a lot of fun, but that's me done with the game*; instead, I thought, *I wish I'd been bigger, faster, stronger, more committed, I wish I'd had more talent, I wish I'd been a bigger part of it.* As such, I still had an itch that needed to be scratched.

Despite almost losing that finger, I actually left school wanting to be a sculptor (yep, a free hit for Hask and Tins) and did an art foundation course in Bournemouth in my gap year. Totem poles were my thing, which would probably see me accused of cultural appropriation nowadays, but like the rugby, it became clear that I was keen but not that able. The totem poles I threatened to erect in my parents' garden 'accidentally' found their way to the bonfire one chilly winter.

Plus, I found my history of art course in Edinburgh a remarkably frustrating experience. I actually tried to switch subjects about two weeks after starting, but was told that I could only swap if I started again the following year. So I ended up losing interest a fortnight into a four-year course and so did just enough to get by, while focusing more on life in the awesome Scottish capital. My sculpting dreams parked, I spent my holidays working out what I should be instead.

I had done a bit of the school Combined Cadet Force, and considered joining the Army. I was quite close to signing-on with the Light Dragoons, who had offered to put me through university, which would have been handy financially. I'm always curious as to what life would have been like if I'd taken the cheque. My oldest mate did cash it, ended up spending six years in the Grenadiers and did two tours of Afghanistan. There is a little bit of me that's jealous of the challenges he faced. Advertising was another option, as was working in the City but, for everything I looked at, all the roads just seemed to lead back to sport, and rugby, of which my knowledge was borderline encyclopedic.

3

I KNEW HOW MUCH HE LOVED ME

HASK

How does one start another book? Do we ease in softly, do we blow the doors off or do we go emotional? As Alex said in his intro, I have told a lot of stories but no one wants to be caught repeating themselves. I have attended enough sportsmen's dinners with ex-rugby players telling the same stories for the last 30 years, until one day I imagine they look up and realise the crowd has no idea what they are talking about. Lucky for you lot, my life is drama, wrapped up in a box of laughter and shrouded in a blanket of chaos, so stories are not something I am short of.

Lots of things have happened since I last put pen to paper and won us an award, and yes it was down to me. Tins never read the first book and was equally as surprised as anyone that we even had a book out or what it contained, and Alex spent so much time flapping over the contents, he almost took off. Talk about constantly being flustered, Alex's heart rate must tick over at 170 bpm all the time. He is like having an agoraphobic, claustrophobic, OCD, depressed, anxious elderly relative who is just constantly worrying. It's very difficult to ever actually get him to a point where he is content, not breathing heavily into a brown paper bag and being attended to by a member of the St John Ambulance.

Now while we didn't get sued from the first book, we did ruffle some feathers, including some feathers close to home. It turns out that perhaps people don't like the truth or would rather remain anonymous when it comes to past actions, but the beauty is you can't argue with the truth.

Don't get me wrong, no one actually spoke to me about anything, as no one ever does, as that requires strength of character and gumption. It's all running off to teacher, or HR, to make complaints, which hold about as much water as a sieve. Luckily, the revolution was quelled with some soft words, some milky tea, and an acknowledgement that your views and feelings were valid. That you were seen and heard, and that those mean words from the bigger boys can't hurt you and you are a special little unicorn living your best life, who should not give it a second thought.

So bearing all this in mind, it's probably time for me to go again and razz a few people up. I mean no one has ever checked in with me to make sure I am OK. When I have been the brunt of scandals or issues, some listed in our first book, some talked about in *What A Flanker*, no one bothered to offer me help, care or advice. No one from management, or staff reached out, I was left with a gut shot in no man's land bleeding out, being eaten alive by angry feminists (not sure there are happy ones, at least not any I've met in 40 years, but I'm happy to be proved wrong), rugby fans, and having my bones picked clean by the media. Just to flag this is of course a joke. I am a feminist myself and I am always happy. So my desire to reach out or back down from someone who got upset by hurty words is non-existent.

It's probably time to cause some more havoc, so sit back and enjoy.

Where do I start? Well, my dad died, which is a pretty big moment in anyone's life, especially mine. Those of you who have read my books will know what an important role he played in my life and how close we were.

While unexpected and tragic, it was not a complete surprise considering the way he lived his life and the health complications he'd had over the last ten years.

My dad was of that generation that will not do anything about medical stuff, is either scared, stupid or a combination of both. I am very different; if there is an issue I get it checked and get it dealt with. I can never understand how you see those people with football-sized tumours on their heads who have just done nothing about it and are shocked and saddened when a doctor finally says either it's terminal or you can't do anything about it without removing half their head. The doctor then usually finishes with these immortal words, 'if only you had come to us sooner'. My dad was very much in that camp.

He had type 2 diabetes, which, after his death, we realised was not being treated by him in the proper way, and it was too late by the time he got fitted with one of those digital monitors in the back of his arm to find his blood sugar was up and down like a yo-yo across the day. You don't have to call in Inspector Morse to solve that mystery – he had clearly not been taking his readings properly, or else doing it only once a day, and then just treating as he thought fit, not following the recommendation of someone who had studied for seven years of medical school, i.e. a doctor.

I mean, you would think when they chopped all his toes off on one foot, bar the big toe, and threatened to take off the whole leg, that internal alarm bells might have started to ring, that perhaps a lifestyle change was in order. Sadly, not for my father, ever the king of just doubling down, who just carried on until the Grim Reaper came a-knocking.

My father, a few weeks before he actually passed, woke up one day with a bladder infection, a chest infection and generally in hell. I would have rushed off to the hospital, but not my dad, he just tried to get on with it. Eventually he was seen by a doctor making a house call who told him the best thing to do was to go to A&E as they could help. He fought my mum as usual, but when he started to piss blood, he perhaps thought that might be where the line was, and he went to the hospital. Now I am not doing down our NHS but what followed was not its proudest outing as an institution. I have to say they have previous in my dad's case, I am not sure if it's due to the part of the world that my parents lived in or maybe it was an exception. My personal experience of the NHS has always been generally positive, but last year when my dad was ill, he was taken to hospital and I found him sitting in a corridor, surrounded by scenes of carnage. The ward was five or six beds deep, people everywhere in various states. Some in the process of expelling bodily fluids from different orifices, others crying for help, others asleep, others I am pretty sure were dead or not far from it. It was fucking horrific, the doctors and nurses run ragged, no idea what was really going on, losing paperwork, forgetting to come back to people, others taking days to get results. I had never seen anything like it. My dad was on a bed, went to the loo, the bed was taken and he was given a chair. He was in there for three days, and it was only halfway through day two that they finally got him another bed. I was shocked – as sportsmen we often got private health care, so this was a big eye-opener.

This time round for my father was not much better. After checking himself in at A&E they triaged him a couple of times, but essentially he was left for over 48 hours in corridors or transferred to other places to then be left with no answers or help. My dad, severely fed up and feeling like shit, just came home. He texted my mum saying it was one of the most hellish 48 hours he had ever experienced and was no closer to being better.

That Thursday night he was clearly not well. He went to bed and sometime in the night he had a small stroke. He woke up with slurred speech and his face had dropped. After his previous experience at A&E, he refused to go back in, they called the paramedics who checked him over, made sure he was OK but told him to go in and get checked properly. However, he would not listen and stayed at home. My mother called me up to say that the side of his face had dropped, and I of course was like, fucking hell, Mum, that's a stroke. I called him up and told him to go in but as always he didn't listen. He did however cough really badly down the phone which sounded like he had some terrible infection on his chest, which was getting worse not better.

Among the other things my dad had done to not aid his wellbeing was to develop an immunity to antibiotics by picking and choosing when he took them and how much of them. 'Oh I have a cold, let me take it for two days then stop' or 'The doctor has given me this for an infection, I will take the dose, hold on it's getting better, I'll stop.' I mean you could not make it up. I have no idea what was going through his head with all this stuff.

I couldn't get down to see him on the Saturday as I had work, but I had a gut feeling this was not going to end well. It was my weekend with my daughter Bodhi so I took her down with me on the Sunday to see him. My dad was in bed when I got there, so I waited for him to come limping down the stairs on his six toes. Like my mum had said, his face had dropped and his speech was a bit slurred, which didn't seem good. But we had a nice day chatting and catching up, we sat in the sun and I filled my parents in on life, divorce updates and general news. I was on my phone a bit that day, fighting a few other fires, which I now regret after what happened that night.

I had to leave around 4.30 p.m. to get back home and put my daughter to bed. So I said to my dad, 'I love you, I am sorry you are feeling like hell, and are having such a shit time of it. Please look after yourself and get checked as you have clearly had some pretty big medical event.' I told Bodhi to give her grandad a big kiss and a hug. I kissed my dad bye as always and drove home, got Bodhi ready for bedtime and read to her her favourite story, *The Tiger Who Came to Tea*, but I change the words in the story as she thinks the pictures are of her, me and Chloe. So it's always Bodhi's mummy this, and Bodhi couldn't have a bath because the tiger had drunk all the water out of the taps. Cheeky fucking tiger, if it was my house, the fucker would not have drunk all of Daddy's beer or eaten all of Daddy's dinner. He would have been told to fuck off and go visit the neighbour's house as he was taking the piss after eating the cupboards bare.

I woke up early on Monday, sorry let me rephrase that: Bodhi woke up early as is her want. She always comes for a cuddle and tries her best to go back to sleep but that only lasts five mins before she starts, 'Daddy, can I have milk; Daddy, can we go downstairs; Daddy, there is a crocodile in my room; Daddy, your dragon Archie (long story not for this book) is he still in the attic – can we go see him?' I got ready for my day, and sorted the house out.

Bodhi was collected by Chloe and I went to the gym. I had a really good training session, I was full of energy, happy with life and had a spring in my step as I emerged from out of the gym into the morning sunshine. (I'd gone through a mad body transformation – dropping from 120kg down to 107kg, got shredded, a new lid and new set of front teeth. People have used the words 'midlife crisis', or 'a cry for help' – I say 'midlife glow-up'. And it's gone down extremely well 'across the board' – I have never had more heat in my life, if you get my drift. It's harder to go home on my own at the moment! I joke, of course – I am not that kind of guy, but if I was then it would almost be unfair.)

Then my phone went and it was my brother, who never calls me.

I answered and he told me that Dad had had a huge stroke in the night and he'd had to do chest compressions. He said it was not good and Dad was fucked. Like proper fucked. He was probably not going to make it to lunch.

I didn't panic or scream. When a month before my mum called me and said dad was having his leg chopped off, I admit I let out an involuntary gasp and a 'no way'. This time I was calmer. I called my PA who cancelled my work for the day, then rang Chloe and my best mate Paul Doran-Jones (for him my dad was like a second father). I also called a very nice doctor from the private sector and said I wanted to move heaven and earth to get my dad into a private ward. I went home and showered and drove two hours to see him.

When I turned up at the hospital, he was paralysed completely down one side, his face had dropped even further, he couldn't speak, couldn't swallow, and one eye was half-closed. He could, ironically, give a thumbs-up, that was it. He was in a bad way but at least awake, which was a surprise.

I am not sure he had any idea who I was or what was going on. Mum and my brother seemed to think he did, but he never showed any signs of recognition or happiness to see me. It was like he had been reset. Mum, bless her, kept trying to interpret what he wanted when he motioned or reached for something, but she kept getting it wrong.

'Oh, he's reaching out to you, he knows you are there and he's trying to hold your hand.'

'No, Mum, he's not. He wants some water!'

At which point my dad would then nod or give a thumbs-up.

Mum would say, 'Oh look, he wants you to come closer.'

'No, Mum, he wants to have a piss,' to which he would nod again.

It was actually very funny in a way. That's my way of dealing with things, using dark humour, so I made jokes about it. The more Mum got it wrong, the more my brother and I took the piss.

I told my mum that it turns out that even after decades of marriage you still don't know what he wants. Or maybe now that Dad was trapped in his own body, she was belatedly getting revenge? I could see her unplugging the battery in his wheelchair if he ever got that far or making him sit through all the TV shows he would never let her watch. 'What's that, Jonathan, you want to watch the omnibus edition of *Antiques Roadshow*?' Then Mum throws her voice and like a ventriloquist pretends to be my dad and says, 'Yes, Susie, that would be lovely,' all the while my dad is looking wild eyed and unable to speak, knowing he can't escape, and thinking *Fuck my life* as the theme tune kicks in for eight hours of old people pretending they aren't interested in the value of anything and would never sell. Which we all know is bullshit.

Now having a sick father is not a nice place to be, but having a sick father who was wrapped up in a number of legal battles, court cases and who had money issues, made life even harder. I knew this day was coming where he would go and leave a shit show, I had warned him about all this, but both him and my mum just carried on anyway. So on the day he was taken to the hospital and was unable to function anymore, I officially took over the whole thing. It's no exaggeration to say that since I opened the Pandora's box of my dad's emails, I have not stopped fighting fires and shovelling shit. I am currently sitting in Reno airport waiting to get picked up for Burning Man some three months later and I am still in the midst of drama, wrapped up in a calamity served in a box of hell.

Anyway back to the point, so picture this: I have gone and seen my father who is pretty broken in hospital, at the same time, I am having to start calling lawyers as they are going to start winding up proceedings on one of the companies, with deadlines looming or expired already, while I have to call another three sets of lawyers to tell them that my father is now unable to speak and doesn't really know what day of the week it is and they need to get me up to speed. To date there are four court cases pending and I am now having to sort them.

I know it was important to see my dad, but to be honest there was nothing I could really do for him. We tried to see if he could write but he couldn't really. We got an alphabet up on screen for him to spell stuff out, but it made no sense. What we saw and what he saw must have been very different. I have no idea how it had affected him because he couldn't speak. Strokes affect people very differently, so you just don't know. I realised that I was better served dealing with all this court stuff, business issues and financial worries instead of just sitting in hospital watching my mother trying her hardest to guess what my dad wanted, and him looking in hell, just wanting water that he could not swallow or drink, which itself must have been torture and not something I would wish on anyone. I said goodbye, told him that I loved him and left. Thank God for ChatGPT, because I had to dictate a lot of letters in the car as I was driving back, and get them sent off to various people. I was so caught up in all this that I never really had a chance to let the situation sink in. My brother and I had our own issues to deal with, while my mum was dealing with watching her husband of 40 years struggling in the worst possible ways.

I went back to London and didn't visit again for another week. He was stable, not really changing or showing any signs of improvement, and was waiting to have loads of tests done including MRIs of the brain, CT scans and tests on his heart. So rather than sitting in silence or talking at him, which I didn't want to do, I just worked away and tried to re-arrange the deckchairs on the *Titanic* as it sank around me.

About a week and a half later, I was with my video guy Kallum, getting fitted for a morning suit for Ascot races, when I got a text to call my mum. I got in the car and spoke to Mum on speaker phone in front of Kallum. She basically said that Dad was making no progress, tests on his heart showed it was working at only 15 per cent, and the chest infection was in fact pneumonia, which meant he had been having his lungs suctioned multiple times every day because of the build-up of fluid, which was horrific for him. He was unable to eat or swallow, he was being fed through a tube, and they basically wanted to stop treating him and just make him comfortable.

Mum, my brother and I had previously talked about my dad's situation, about the state he was in and how much he would hate being like this, that he would not want to live if this was what he had to experience for the rest of his life, so we had to decide whether to sign a Do Not Resuscitate (DNR) order. This was not a conversation I ever thought I would have with my father awake in the next room. You can never imagine saying that you don't want someone to help one of your loved ones if they are fighting for their lives. Part of me felt it was all a bit callous, as if we'd decided that we just couldn't be bothered waking him up. But honestly, looking at him and knowing him, this is not the life he would have wanted; he would have hated it, of that I am certain.

I was not sure what to say to Mum. I asked what she meant about stopping treatment. 'Basically,' she said hurriedly, 'the doctors said he won't get better with all these complications; if it was just the stroke, maybe, but the rest of it and the heart failing, he was never going to recover.' In short, they wanted to stop treatment and start palliative care.

Now I thought what was being inferred was that they would put him on an ascending dose of morphine until eventually he drifted off. For example they would start the treatment on the Friday, and then call the family and get them in over the weekend to say their last goodbyes and then by Sunday night he'd probably be gone peacefully in his sleep. I said to Mum that I would need to speak to the doctor and understand what was going on before I agreed to stop treating my dad; it's one thing not to resuscitate him, it's another thing to just let him die. Poor Kallum did not know what to say or do, he heard the whole thing, I told him I needed to go right away, and he just gave me a hug and said, 'I am here for you.' I then drove back to the hospital.

So when I arrived at the hospital expecting Dad to be at death's door, imagine my surprise as I walked into the ward and there he was awake and giving me a thumbs-up. *What the fuck is going on?* I thought. We were agreeing to put him out of his misery and the next minute he was awake and seemed like he was on day one.

My mum was sitting by his side, and my brother was lurking somewhere. I walked over and held Dad's hand but he couldn't grip it properly. He'd never really showed any signs of affection once he was in hospital, whereas normally he was a loving father. Which in itself made things harder and made me think he didn't really know what was going on and that his brain had gone haywire.

I thought, *I'm not agreeing to give my dad a nudge towards death when he still seems to be aware of his surroundings.* He kept signalling for water which he couldn't drink, you could only wet his lips or try to put a tiny spoonful into his mouth, which he couldn't then swallow so it dribbled out. It was hell to watch. It was like all he could think about was drinking. When I asked if he was in pain, had a headache or needed the loo, he shook his head. He just wanted water. I signalled to my mum for us to have a chat in the corridor.

'What is going on?' I said. 'He seems just like when I left him a week ago.' She agreed it was very strange, so I said we needed to see a doctor and have a chat as I wasn't agreeing to anything until I understood what was going on.

Eventually, we tracked the top doctor down, and the three of us were ushered into a family room. You could only imagine the tragic things that had been discussed in there.

The doctor basically confirmed that while Dad was a fighter he just had too many things wrong with him. Even the diabetic ulcers on his feet had started to get worse, everything was just getting on top of him and he would, in her opinion, never return to normality or anything close to it. If it had been one or two issues and a stroke then fair enough, but all of them together underpinned with diabetes and the results of the brain scan which showed he'd had two major strokes, spelt the end. She did say that if he had come in on the Friday when he had the mini episode/stroke, they could have treated him or the clot and probably prevented what happened next.

This was so galling to hear and just made me more frustrated with him, because if he hadn't been so stubborn and did what he was told he would not have been in this state of hell at the age of 69.

Her conclusion was that with all these things, treatment would not really work, and that while yes he was fighting, the fight was going out of him. They felt that the best thing they could do was stop treatment and make him comfortable. I asked if he'd be gone that night, to which she replied no. I asked if he might rally, to which she replied yes, but that he was never going to get any better.

I did keep saying to the doctor that he seemed fine next door or no worse than a week ago. I did not want to agree to stop treating someone who could get better. She said that yes while he had perked up this afternoon, he had been bad this morning and not great last night. She said that Dad was a fighter, that every morning she would come and see him and he would give a thumbs up, and would sit through the horrific suction of his lungs and other things, with a form of energy and vibe. However she added that in the morning he had waved her away, and wanted nothing to do with the treatment, nurses or doctors. That the light and fight were going out of him. I asked if making him comfortable meant basically giving him a nudge with morphine. The doctor said no, not at all. It was about stopping treatment and making him comfortable; he could last a few days or maybe two weeks, or there was a minute chance he would rally, but she said it was near-on impossible and if he did, his life would never get back to anything that resembled normal. He would never work nor probably speak again.

So Mum, my brother and I had to have another summit on our own once the doctor left the room. It was the oddest conversation I have ever had, basically talking about letting my father die, what we would do when it happened, what we would do about the funeral, every implication, while he was in the other room oblivious to any of this. I did keep making the point that he seemed OK and that we would need to keep an eye on him, and questioned whether the doctors were jumping the gun a bit on cutting off the treatment.

In the end, we agreed to let the nurses withdraw treatment and just make him as comfortable as possible for however long he lasted.

We didn't mention any of this to Dad when we filed back into his ward, we all just pretended like things were normal. I am not sure really what we should have done, it was like a big horrible secret that Dad wasn't in on. My brother announced he was going to buy some fruit from the vendor at the front of the hospital. I'd never seen a fruit and veg seller operate out front, but this one did a good trade as it was always busy. I forgot Dad couldn't talk, so started asking him things only to remember he couldn't reply, and Mum just busied herself, adjusting his bed, and suggesting things that he clearly didn't want. So business as usual, until an energetic woman popped out of nowhere and said, 'Hi you must be Jonathan, I'm the palliative care nurse.' I looked at Dad and was convinced his one good eye bulged in its socket and started rotating round to look at Mum and me as if to say, 'What. The. Fuck', because he'd basically just been told he was dying. It was the worst surprise ever! It was straight out of a scene from the TV series *After Life* or a *Carry On* movie.

I gave the nurse an evil look and the tightest smile you have ever seen – my lips were so tight you could not have fitted a Rizla between them. I mouthed, 'Shut up,' and gesticulated with my eyes for her to leave the room, and Mum said to her, 'I think you've got the wrong person.'

'No, no, no,' said the nurse, 'Jonathan Haskell.'

'No, you've definitely got the wrong person …' I eventually shooed the nurse into the corridor and said, 'We haven't told him!' It was darkly comical, but it must have been terrifying for my poor dad.

Before going home that day, I went back in to see Dad, told him I loved him, kissed him on the head and said I would be back in a day or so. I said goodbye. He couldn't say he loved me back, but I knew he did because he'd told me many times before then.

I have done so much therapy and spoken to so many people about death and losing loved ones over the years that one of the common themes that I had heard was that people always wished they had said they loved someone more, or at all. Or if they could have one more conversation, they would tell that person how much they meant to them. For my last book, *Approach Without Caution*, we looked into what people said on their deathbeds and it was never, 'I wish I had more cars, more houses,' it was more time with loved ones and friends, and that they wanted to say things they never had or should have said more.

Due to all this, over the last six years or so as my folks got older I would always tell them I loved them on phone calls or in person. It was very important to me, especially the way my father lived at 100 mph and hit it hard in all areas. I always had this day in the back of my mind, so I didn't want any regrets.

My dad was a force. Undeniably charismatic, unapologetically opinionated, and at times utterly infuriating. But never boring. He had presence. He filled a room, and he knew it. But what I always found so fascinating, and something I didn't fully appreciate until I was older, is how multi-layered he was. He had this 'lads' lad' exterior – jokes, charm, full of bravado – but underneath all that was a man of enormous feeling. A romantic. A softie. A worrier. Someone who felt everything deeply, but didn't always show, or even know how to show it, in obvious ways.

Once, on a long car journey, just the two of us, my dad opened up about something I've never forgotten. It wasn't dramatic, it wasn't overly emotional, but it stuck with me. He explained that the reason he was always so supportive of my brother and me, the reason he always turned up, always forgave, and always pushed us to be our best, was because his dad didn't.

His dad wasn't there in the way he needed him to be. And that left a mark. So my dad made a choice – a quiet, powerful decision – that he was going to do everything his father hadn't. He was going to be present. He was going to be involved. He was going to give us the support and love he'd longed for when he was our age.

And for all the big bravado and booming opinions, that moment of honesty was one of the most vulnerable things I'd ever seen from him. And it told me everything I needed to know about who he was.

Because, you see, he didn't just become a great father by accident. He chose to be one.

He was always better at articulating himself in letters and emails than he was perhaps in person. I always kissed him on the cheek when I saw him and gave him a hug. We had always done it since I was little. The same with my mum. The only time he tried to change this was in the Spirit of Rugby room, after an England game. He was with some alickadoos in blazers and was clearly showing off or trying to ingratiate himself with these old duffers, who hang around post-match functions like seagulls outside a chip van. As I approached him he put his hand out to shake mine, presumably because he was a bit self-conscious in front of all the old bastards, or perhaps he defaulted to his public school ways. I laughed and said, 'Fuck off, Dad, why you trying to shake my hand?' He got all flustered – 'Oh, sorry, son' – and promptly gave me a kiss and a hug. You see, I think there is nothing more manly than being yourself and being vulnerable. Being strong and tough is not about acting strong and tough, it's the ability to have depth and range to yourself. Kissing my dad on the cheek and being affectionate makes me more of a man than some muppet who thinks it's odd or weak. I can hand on heart say I am able to always express how I feel, and if I am struggling, saying I am and doing something about it is more powerful than the guy who lies, puts on a character and then ultimately ends up messing up his life because he couldn't be honest or vulnerable.

I once kissed him in front of two older public school lads who were in the England team when I was first selected at 21, and they started calling me gay. You know how it goes: 'Oi, Haskell, stop snogging your fucking dad. Haskell, you gay kissing your old man,' etc. All top-level chat as you can see. I said to them, 'Lads, I think you're a bit confused. First of all, that would be incest, but let's not quibble about the details. Just because you two first met your dads on your 18th birthdays, when you were finally released from your Swiss boarding school, not everyone is emotionally repressed.'

I actually saw these guys with their dads a few times and it was just as I imagined. The mum was given a hug, in one case the dad just nodded at his son, with his hands firmly behind his back, and the other was given a strong handshake and that was it. You could not pay me to have that kind of relationship with my father. The whole thing screamed emotional repression. I will never be anything but loving and affectionate with my daughter. I will always tell her how much I love her and always be affectionate, without bordering on embarrassing – but all parents go through that phase when they are the last person their kid wants to see or hang around with. You will know from my other books how much my parents were liked by my mates and how I would often, in later life, take them out or get them involved in events and parties. You only get one set of parents – treasure them.

Having left the hospital after basically agreeing to let my father die, my head was full of *what's going to happen next*, and *how do we sort all these problems out*. Ironically one of the court cases my father had been fighting, against a landlord for gross negligence, we won and a settlement offer came in as I was in the car. Which was good news in some ways, but sad that my dad had been fighting it for four years and would never know. I then had the job of having to sort lawyers' fees and creditors out of that money, which may have meant there was actually nothing left for anyone, including myself and my mother who were both investors in the business.

You would think after a traumatic day like this, one might want to relax or spend time with loved ones or friends. Not me. I spent the rest of that day emptying my parents' storage unit, which was quite a task. It turns out Dad hadn't thrown anything away for 40 years, and he had ended up paying roughly £4k a month in storage fees – which is barking mad money – only to run out of space and have to get a mate to let him store it in a huge barn at his logging and wood re-finery business. However, the stuff had been there almost a year, and because of Dad's ill health and the fact that he was a control freak and would not let anyone go in there, the stuff was untouched. I had no idea any of this was going on until my mum said we had three weeks to get rid of all this stuff, some of it valuable, some of it not seen for decades.

I mean, I operate a policy: if I haven't used it in a year I am never going to use it, so I give it away or sell it. Not my parents. They decided to keep everything, which for me is mental behaviour. When I turned up I could not believe the size of the building – it was like an aircraft hangar. The amount of shit in this barn was insane. I must have got through about 300 boxes and built a mound of rubbish bigger than the whole of the downstairs of my house.

I had salvaged lots of stuff to sell and discovered that he had framed all my MOM awards for England and Wasps, my shirts and my Heineken Cup medals, etc. I knew he had done some of it but not all of it. I found my entire career in boxes. It was all there, in those boxes, along with loads of memorabilia from other parts of my career. There was an England shirt from every game I played, from every age-group, all the shirts I had swapped, and programmes from every game. There were also scrapbooks of newspaper cuttings. I was there from 11 a.m. to 10 p.m. at night and was not even a quarter of the way through before I had to go to bed.

The following morning, I went back to the hospital, expecting to find Dad nice and comfortable as we had seen him the day before. But when I walked in, he was not in his normal bed on the ward. I thought initially he had died in the night and no one had told us, then I saw him at the end in a room with glass walls. I walked over. I was met with a chaotic scene. He was burning up with what looked to be a fever, panting like a dog, unable to breathe, his chest rattling, his one functioning eye staring at the ceiling. It was horrific, like he was a completely different person, as if he was in hell again. I had to do everything in my power not to cry and my mum, normally very stoic, started panicking that this wasn't right, he shouldn't be like this.

I looked around for help and found a nurse. 'You've got to do something, this isn't right, does he look comfortable to you?' He said he had been given morphine. I said, 'Well give him more, he has a fever, this is not comfortable, this is fucking awful.'

My dad was there in body but that was about it. It was one of the worst things I have seen up-close. He was just fighting for air and not responding, even if you held his hand. I didn't really know what to do, but I had to be strong for my brother and mum who were finding it terrible, because it was. I put wet towels on the back of his head and neck and held his hand. We stayed there for about 20 minutes and tried to make him calmer. You couldn't give him water because he would choke. There was nothing else we could do.

I knew I had all this legal stuff to sort, and I was better served being elsewhere. I said to my mum and brother that I should go back to London as I had Bodhi and my actual day job, among sorting out the other disasters I had been left with. They said alright and would report back if anything changed.

Before I left I held my dad's hand, kissed him on the head and said, 'Thank you so much for being an amazing dad. I appreciate everything you did for me, I owe you more than words can say. I love you.' And I left. I wasn't sure that I would see him alive again, but I hoped that if they made him comfortable he might regain consciousness and things would be calmer for a while.

My mum and my brother did return the next day, and they found him asleep, his breathing had slowed down and he was peaceful, he was no longer burning up and he was calm. I had intended to come back the day after, but around 2 p.m. I got a call from my mum and as soon as I saw her name on the phone I knew what it meant.

Dad had died peacefully in his sleep. It had been two whole weeks since the stroke. He was seemingly not in pain. He'd had a good life and had lived it to the max, but he was only 69, which is no age at all.

I wish I could change my final memory of Dad as it's not how I want to remember him, but at least I didn't feel like there was anything left unsaid between us. I'm glad Bodhi and I went and had lunch with him the previous Sunday and that she got to say goodbye. I am not sure she will ever remember him, sadly, but that's the way it goes.

I haven't spent much time thinking about our relationship since he died, probably because I was at peace with how we left things. I was honest about how much I loved him and what a great dad I thought he was, and I knew how much he loved me and how incredibly proud he was of my achievements, so there's nothing really to examine.

There's that saying that when it comes to grief, the cheque is in the post, and friends keep checking in on me, because they assume that my upbeat demeanour is just a front.

Maybe I will have a meltdown at some stage, but while I do have moments when I think, 'I should tell Dad about this' or 'I need to give my dad a call', before remembering that he's no longer around, I think I'll be OK. It's Mum I'm worried about because they were together for 45 years, and while she's a very strong, independent and sociable woman, I know she's had tough, lonely days. I check in with her all the time and we speak most days.

Dad was loud, brash, funny, outgoing and certainly not everyone's cup of tea. He was an eternal optimist, always believing things would pan out alright.

You don't get to be someone like my dad without leaving a bit of rubble in your wake. He had strong views. He held grudges. He was allergic to being told what to do. But more often, he was the one standing up for someone, fighting a corner, demanding fairness, and if he clashed with someone, it's probably because they were being an arse. And, quite often, they were.

He worked tirelessly for us. For me, for my brother, and for Mum. Everything he did, everything he chased, was for us. He wanted to give us the childhood he didn't have. And he succeeded.

And my God, he had standards. Everything had to be done just so. A Sunday in our house before guests came over was never a relaxing affair. It was a military operation. Lawns mowed within an inch of their lives, leaves swept, fences painted. The entire house, inside and out, had to be pristine. It was as if we were hosting a royal garden party.

But that was Dad. No half measures. If a job's worth doing, it's worth doing properly. That was one of his many mantras. We heard it so often it might as well have been embroidered on our school jumpers.

He was also incredibly clever. Razor-sharp. He could argue his case with the best of them, often long after everyone else had given up. He should have been a barrister, no question. He had an amazing ability to distil a complicated issue into something clear, digestible, and usually wildly persuasive. Except when it came to things like the dishwasher, cooking or flat-pack furniture, then the swear words came out and we were all told to 'bugger off unless we were going to help' or 'just leave it as you are doing it wrong'. Classic Dad.

And when I think about the things he taught me beyond the anecdotes and mottos, it really comes down to one fundamental idea: integrity. He used to say, 'You can lie to everyone else, but you can't lie to yourself.' And it didn't make sense to me when I was younger. But as I got older, especially when I started navigating my career, stepping into the public eye, I realised how important that lesson was. In a world where people pretend, where everything is curated and filtered and spun, Dad's words kept me grounded. They forced me to be honest, especially with myself. And I think, more than any coaching session, more than any motivational quote, that shaped me into the person I am today.

He wasn't perfect. None of us are. He could be stubborn, unreasonable, and, in his later years, a bit of a hoarder as I have mentioned, although my mum tells me that came from growing up without much. He went to Wellington, surrounded by privilege and polish, and I think part of him always felt like he had to prove something. And he did. He built businesses. He made a life. He gave us everything.

He was never great at dealing with problems and internalised a lot of them. I have alluded to the shit show he left. I think he thought he could just keep fighting and dodging and robbing Peter to pay Paul and it would all work out in the end.

Some parents leave their kids lots of nice stuff. My old man left me a shitload of stress.

He was so deeply invested in me, in my success, in my happiness, that when things didn't go well, he couldn't hide it. His face would give him away instantly. And it wasn't easy, especially for someone like me, because he could come across as critical. Direct. Blunt, even. There were times when I'd come off a pitch thinking I'd given everything, and he'd be waiting there, ready to dissect it all like a post-mortem. Every ruck, every missed tackle, every yellow card.

And I know now, even if I didn't already know it then, that it all came from a place of love. He never thought he was doing anything but the best for me. But sometimes it was a bit much. As I got older, I had to say, 'Dad, just … let it breathe. Let the whistle settle before we go into analysis mode.'

I'll always be grateful to Chloe, the mother of my wonderful daughter, Bodhi who once pulled him aside after a particularly brutal post-match debrief. She'd seen how despondent I looked, barely five minutes after coming off the field. And she said something simple but vital: 'Just be a bit more positive.' And he took that on board. Because as much as he was set in his ways, if he saw something was hurting the people he loved, he listened.

And that, to me, was a mark of the man. Proud, passionate, sometimes maddening, but always willing to grow. And always, always in my corner.

One of my mates said recently, 'Your dad was the dad of all dads.' And it's true. He was the alpha among alphas. There wasn't a bloke alive who could drink with him and not end up horizontal. I remember one poor lad, one of my brother's friends, thought he could go toe-to-toe with Dad on tequila. Big mistake. That kid's father ended up stapling bin-liners to the inside of the family car before driving him home, just to protect the leather.

But Dad was outrageous, generous, and always completely himself. Behind the chaos was always kindness. Even when things were hard for him, he still made time for others. He still helped quietly, without asking for anything in return.

In his final years, I watched him fight a different kind of battle against his own body, against the stress that built up over a lifetime of pushing, striving, worrying. And even when he wasn't well, he showed up. For me, for our family, for his friends. That, above all else, is what I'll remember. He showed up

In many ways, he was a textbook example of his generation: the kind of man who would rather suffer in silence than admit something was wrong. He could be in excruciating pain and still insist everything was absolutely fine. And if he finally did go to the doctor, he'd charm the socks off everyone and pretend he'd just popped in for a chat.

Honestly, I don't know if it was fear, or pride, or just a lifelong habit of not wanting to burden anyone. But whatever it was, he wore it like armour.

Every nurse, doctor, consultant, and porter adored him. And I mean, adored. It's quite something when the district nurse who's been looking after your feet for months turns up at the hospital just to see you and tells the kids to stay in the car while she does it. Or when the paramedics who've lifted you off the bathroom floor are still laughing about what you said on the way to A&E. Or the firemen (firemen!) are talking about how funny you were, even while you were half-immobile and they had to carry you out of the house after taking off the staircase bannister.

That was Dad. His legs could be falling off, and he'd still be trying to crack a joke, lighten the mood, make someone smile. It was like he couldn't help himself. That spark that irreverent, irresistible charm never went away. Right to the end, he was still making people laugh. Still putting others at ease, even while he wasn't.

And that, I think, tells you everything about him.

There were some stressful times when he managed me early in my career, in terms of finances: 'Brand Haskell', something that I think he invented or led to the invention of through conversations with Ian McGeechan. We did grow slightly further apart after that. Male ego is a real thing, especially in men of his vintage, and he found it difficult to put his hand up and say, 'Maybe I don't have the answers', but nothing he ever did was malicious.

*　*　*

Dad's funeral was a fine celebration of his life, mixed with farcical elements that wouldn't have been out of place in a Richard Curtis film.

Dad was always late, because he was always trying to spin too many plates at once. In that tradition, my brother was still in the shower ten minutes before we were meant to be at the crematorium, which I'd just discovered was 25 minutes away.

I was telling Edward to hurry the fuck up, Mum was running around panicking, and when Edward finally made it downstairs, he demanded a couple of tequila shots. I couldn't find any tequila, but I did find a dusty quarter bottle of Lamb's Rum, so he had a couple of lugs of that instead. We made it to the crematorium with a couple of minutes to spare.

Because we wanted it to be a celebration of Dad's life, everyone came dressed in colourful clothes, including my old Stade Français team-mate Ollie Phillips, who wore a pink Stade hoodie, similar to one that Dad had. Everything was going swimmingly until a nurse who treated Dad went to hug my mum, leaned on the pew thinking it was fixed to the floor but it wasn't, and almost collapsed on top of her. This nurse was wobbling around like a Weeble, a couple of people were trying to right her, someone else was peeling the pew off my mum, my brother was sobbing, and I was trying to be the light of the family and hold things together.

One of Dad's best friends from school said a few words and did an amazing job of summing up his character. Harry Holden sat next to him in class for years, and his underlying theme was that wherever Jonathan Haskell was, there was trouble (whenever Dad's name was mentioned in company, people would either laugh and say, 'What a lad', or visibly pale; and when I first turned up at Wellington, ancient teachers would say to me, 'What's your name, boy?', I'd tell them, and they'd reply, 'Oh God, you're not related to Jonathan Haskell, are you?').

We had what you might describe as a 'progressive' vicar, who was a bit happy-clappy and made the mistake of saying after Harry's speech, 'I don't think anyone can beat that, that's the best speech ever!' He then lunged in with, next up we have a lady called Sheila, who is going to say a few words. What an intro. To be fair, Sheila is not easily rattled.

She had worked for my dad for 20 years and was a dear friend of the family, was next up on the lectern, and she actually spoke brilliantly. Sheila told the story of the time Dad was commissioned to make gifts for the Priory rehab hospital, and he came up with the idea of tea towels and aprons bearing the legend, I CLEANED UP AT THE PRIORY. Everyone else was obviously against it, but Dad stuck to his guns, they ended up being massive sellers and he made a fortune. Then there was the time Dad marched into the office one day and said, 'Sheila, you need to get me to Mars!' 'Blimey, Jonathan, I'm good, but not even I can do that!' He didn't mention that he was talking about the Mars factory in Slough, and it wouldn't surprise me if Sheila spent the rest of the day googling space shuttles, such was her loyalty.

I really wanted my eulogy to be special, and my biggest concern was getting through it without breaking down, because that would have been a waste. Thankfully, it went really well. Too often when someone dies, people only want to talk about their good side, but I thought it was important to mention Dad's flaws as well. What makes people interesting is that they're multi-dimensional. Mum was blown away by it.

As the vicar was doing his 'ashes to ashes, dust to dust' bit, very theatrically, he started backing away towards the coffin that was behind him, he bumped his hip on the coffin and gave out a high-pitched 'aah!', much like the so-called 'Aah Girl' on the internet (there's a clip of her bumping her hip on a bedpost and going 'aah', which people have cut into various songs). He styled it out without any pain showing but it must have killed him. Little moments like that seem particularly funny at funerals and I very nearly lost my shit while my brother just scowled. My favourite bit was when the vicar did a very camp dust to dust and mimed the actions over the coffin. He did a great job and it was a really nice service but laced with some real humorous bits. To be fair, Dad would not have minded; he and I were always pissing ourselves hysterical at funerals, we couldn't help it, it was either Dad's God-awful singing or someone doing something that had us in stitches.

The bit from this funeral that really got me going was when Harry told a story about my dad, where he and Dad both got into a load of trouble, and Harry was pretty sure that my dad sold him out to the teachers. If you cast your mind back to my previous books *What A Flanker* or *Ruck Me* there is a story about Dozza (my mate Paul Doran-Jones) and me making a porno at school which had terrible consequences. The culmination of this story was that after intense pressure and some Machiavellian tricks I came clean to the teachers and shopped Dozza.

When Harry said this, I turned to find Dozza who was in attendance at the funeral looking at me, and he shouted, 'I knew it's a family full of snitches, it's in their blood!' Those who knew the story were laughing to tears.

After the service we were invited to say our final good-byes to the coffin before walking out. My mum wanted us to be the first at the reception to greet people so we left sharpish. I put my hand on the coffin, said 'I love you, Dad' and then walked out. I wanted to stay and say hello, but these cremation places run on a conveyor belt system and we were late so the next mourners were waiting and guys were freaking out that things were running behind. My satnav said the George and Dragon, where the wake was being held, was 22 minutes away, which sounded about right. But as we were driving through Amberley, Mum suddenly said, 'Why are we here?' It turned out we were heading to the wrong pub, so we had to turn back, and we turned up at the correct George and Dragon late, hot and flustered. But it was a great do, full of people I hadn't seen for ages, with fun and laughter. Everyone kept saying, 'How come you're late?' and I just said, 'It's what Dad would have wanted.'

I know it's a cliché, but Dad would have loved to be there, as he loved a party. It's always silly that it takes a death to get everyone back together. And once that was over, my best mate Dozza and I went back to Mum's house, as it is now, and got stuck into a few bottles of Dad's decent red wine.

That wasn't ideal, because I had to work the next day, but it was only right and proper.

4

I'M YOUNG, I'M KEEN, I'LL DO ANYTHING

PAYNO

When I was 19, I wrote a letter to Sky Sports, asking if I could come in and do some work experience, and when I didn't hear anything, I wrote another one. And another one. Eventually, they replied, saying they wanted me to show I'd done other things in the industry before thinking about giving me a chance. So I wrote to Bath, my local team, and they invited me in for three or four days.

My time at the Rec was fairly uneventful – I think I wrote short biographies of the players – but I'd supported that club since I was seven or eight, and I was in awe of all those guys – Jeremy Guscott, Ben Clarke, Adedayo Adebayo, Iain Balshaw, Mark Regan, Phil de Glanville, Mike Catt, and a young lad called Mike Tindall – and really quite astonished to be working in the sports industry, if you could call it that.

After my short stint with Bath, I had some work experience lined up with a sports agency in London, only for it to fall through on the Monday morning. That meant I had two weeks to kill in a family friend's flat, but rather than stew, I picked up one of those old blue Thomson directories, flipped straight to sports marketing agencies and started making calls.

I had my spiel – 'I'm young, I'm keen, I'll do absolutely anything, whether it's making tea and coffee or doing the photocopying' – but I got all the way through the agencies beginning with A without any of them biting. The first agency beginning with B was Benchmark Sport, and after I'd given the guy on the other end of the phone my patter, he replied, 'Do you bat or bowl?' 'I don't understand,' I said. 'I suppose I'd bat if I had to.' 'Good,' he replied, 'come to our office at two this afternoon and we'll interview you. If you survive, you can do a couple of weeks with us.'

Benchmark Sport's office was in a mews behind Charlotte Street in the West End, which is where the glamour ended, because it resembled a dungeon. The man I'd spoken to on the phone was Nick Keller, and almost as soon as I arrived, he led me out into the mews, along with five or six colleagues, and we started playing mews cricket. For about 20 minutes, they took turns bowling to me, while asking me questions, and I managed to survive.

Benchmark was a gang of Durham University graduates who looked after top rugby players, including England's Richard Hill and Will Greenwood. They were young, brimming with positivity, and I spent a brilliant two weeks with them, including working on the first ever Sports Industry Awards (which is now a huge event but back then was a couple of hundred people packed into an underground hotel dining room).

Looking back now, it was such a fantastic time to be starting out in the sports industry. The office was a brilliant hive of hilarious chaos, working everything out on the fly and making it up as we went along. Their accountant was called Big Al, for obvious reasons, which meant I was christened Lil' Al. I still see and work with Nick now, 25 years later, and he still greets me so. Because it was quite a tight gang, and I'd got stuck in, I remember being invited to their Christmas party. We were all dressed up in 1970s gear and were set a challenge to buy a Secret Santa present for the office in 30 minutes on Regent's Street. I bombed into Hamley's, jumped into a photo booth, pulled out the double guns and had my photo printed onto a mug. I added 'Happy Christmas, love from Lil Al'. It was still in their kitchen ten years later, and I reckon that mug has got me more work than any business card ever has. The sports industry is enormous, but small at the same time, in that everyone knows someone who knows someone, and Nick gave the right people a nudge at Sky. And now that I had a foot in the door, I began to get really excited.

My first Sky gig was on *Soccer AM*, and my very first task was making a wire leg for one of the show's skits. Those sculpting ambitions came in handy after all. I wasn't the biggest football fan, but the show was at its peak and had an unbelievable energy. It was edgy, irreverent and a bit chaotic, and while it was very of its time – I'd wager that Soccerettes won't be making a comeback on British TV any time soon – it was incredibly influential. Those Saturday mornings were just extraordinary – I remember making a cup of coffee for Mr T in the green room and just wondering how on earth I'd ended up in such a place.

But while *Soccer AM* was a lot of fun to dip into, I was desperate to work in the rugby department, which was just across the corridor. I must have been the only work-experience kid to land a spot on *Soccer AM* and ask for a transfer.

But having got my wish, I was now working in an office with the likes of former Bath fly-half Stuart Barnes, an absolute hero of mine growing up, and former England scrum-half Dewi Morris. It was quite intimidating, but also a very exciting time to arrive at Sky Sports, which was putting so much energy and money into broadcasting in a way that had never been done before in the UK.

The BBC had its tradition, but its sports offering was quite bitty, as typified by *Grandstand*, which might jump from golf to horse racing to rugby league in the space of a couple hours. In contrast, Sky Sports, the noisy disruptor, was offering sporting feasts. Instead of sports fans having to be thankful for what they were given, they could have as much as they wanted.

While Premier League football was the centrepiece of the feast, rugby – domestic, European and international – had a prominent place. Rugby hadn't been professional for long, and it was a very exciting and optimistic time for the sport. England were finally sorting themselves out under Clive Woodward, and the likes of Jonny Wilkinson, Martin Johnson, Jason Robinson and Lawrence Dallaglio were becoming a proper team and household names. The knock-out games in the Heineken Cup were appointment TV, and Super Rugby was a glittering product, with players such as Jonah Lomu, Christian Cullen and Tana Umaga lighting up the screens every week. It really felt like rugby was about to go stratospheric.

Production runners are at the bottom of the broadcasting food chain, and most of my early work at Sky consisted of making tea and coffee, photocopying and collecting sandwiches. That was exactly what I'd signed up for, and I certainly wasn't complaining. But after two weeks of making myself as useful as possible, the rugby department asked me to stay on for two more. I organised interviews with former Lions players, ahead of the 2001 tour to Australia, and was asked to help out on a couple of match days. I was now at the heart of the action, helping to tell stories about the game I loved, even though I was just pushing buttons and plugging in stats (and still fetching drinks). It really was kid at Christmas stuff.

When that initial work experience stint came to an end, I asked the executive producer Martin Turner if I could carry on working for them on the Lions tour, if I could get to Australia under my own steam. Martin was up for that, so I took out a student loan, spent the whole lot on flights and really went for it.

By chance, a couple of mates I was playing with at Edinburgh Accies were travelling down under, so I hooked up with them in Brisbane and we drove all the way to Melbourne and then back up to Sydney, in what I believe was a Nissan Sunny. But on Thursdays, Fridays and Saturdays, I'd work for Sky, helping them prepare for games and mucking in on match days. It was incredibly exciting to be on the other side of the world, working it all out in real time.

The Lions had always been the biggest thing in rugby for me, and I was incredibly lucky to see the first Test of that 2001 tour from pitchside. I was meant to be working the kettle again before sitting in a truck in the bowels of the Gabba, pressing a button every time someone made a tackle or turnover, which is how stats were done back then. But the equipment got detained in customs, so 15 minutes before kick-off, having done all my prep, Martin said to me, 'There's nothing else for you to do, here's a pitchside pass if you want it.'

I can still remember walking up a ramp into the stadium, emerging into the most extraordinary wall of noise and that sea of red-jerseyed Lions fans. I was utterly awestruck. I remember thinking, 'Spending an entire student loan on this was pretty ballsy, but I reckon it's paid off. This might be as good as it ever gets ...' Then the game started, and the Lions produced arguably their greatest performance of the professional era to blow away the reigning world champions. Jason Robinson skipped past Chris Latham for the first try after just three minutes, opposite wing Dafydd James added a second, before tries from Brian O'Driscoll and Scott Quinnell put the Lions out of sight in the second half. The Wallabies scored a couple down the stretch to make the scoreline more respectable, but it was still a comprehensive victory. And sitting there on a plastic chair, yards from the action, I thought, *I want more of this.*

I still had another two years of university, but I did work experience with Sky in every holiday I could. One week, I rolled my ankle in an inter-mural match and tore my ligaments really badly, and I was meant to be working for Sky the following day. My ankle was black and blue and swollen up like a balloon, but I hobbled to the station, caught the train down to London, got the Tube from King's Cross to Earl's Court, and hobbled from Earl's Court to Chelsea, where I was staying with a mate. I didn't arrive until two in the morning, he wasn't there and didn't answer my calls, so I slept in the stairwell outside his flat. I was dragging my foot like Kevin Spacey in *The Usual Suspects* for the next few days, but that's how committed I was to breaking into sports broadcasting.

Having said that, there was obviously still a part of me that thought it was all a bit of a pipe dream, because I did apply for jobs in other industries. Luckily for me, I got found out at my first interview in the City. The opening question of the interview was 'What did you get in your A-levels?' Not a tricky question, except for the fact that the CV I'd sent the investment bank in advance showed that I had three As and a B. But the CV I gave them on the day showed, correctly, that I had two As and two Bs. I really can't tell you why I lied in the first place, why I changed it back, or why I blamed being pranked by one of my flat-mates. But my career in finance was over after one question.

They might have chucked me out, but instead they asked me what else I was interested in, and I told them about my work at Sky and going on a Lions tour. When I was done, one of the interviewers said to me, 'Listen, you've got a proper passion. Don't work in the City. It's clear what you want to do, go after it.' What great advice that was. I wasn't even very good with numbers.

Thankfully, Sky offered me a full-time job as a production runner a week after leaving university, in the summer of 2003. And while I honestly don't spend too long worrying about other people's perceptions of me, I think it's important to emphasise that I worked bloody hard to get that gig.

Hask and Tins are constantly giving me stick because I went to Eton (despite the fact they're not exactly urchins, having both attended public school themselves and one being a member of the royal family), but I have a very simple take on what some might call my Eton privilege: I was unbelievably lucky, I'm very grateful to the place and I'm afraid I'm not going to apologise for it. At 13, I didn't really make the decision and in truth I had no real understanding of what I was stepping into, but I know my parents made huge sacrifices to give their children those opportunities, and I'm very grateful for that.

I can't change it, I wouldn't change it, and I'm not going to spend time worrying about it, because it's part of my journey. I didn't get into Sky because I knew the 'right' people, I got in because I kept knocking on doors and didn't stop until they opened. In any walk of life, you need to be in the right place at the right time to be chosen – the luck part – but you also need to graft to be in that right place.

I could have put my feet up for two weeks instead of trawling through that Thomson's Directory and hammering the phone; I could have earned a wage during my holidays, instead of working for Sky for free; I could have done a lot of other things with that student loan; I missed countless birthday parties and holidays because I was working most weekends. But every time I said no to an invitation – a surf trip on such-and-such a date, a wedding in such-and-such a place – I was happy to, because I loved what I'd be doing instead.

It's no different to trying to make it as a sportsperson: lots of people want it, but do they want to do all the work that might enable it to happen? I certainly didn't have it or want it as a player, but like those who do make it as a professional, I went for it in broadcasting.

5

NOT VERY FAST, CAN'T PASS, CAN'T KICK

TINS

To tell the truth, I'd imagined starting my career at a less fashionable club than Bath – Gloucester or Newcastle, for example. I'd always seen myself as a bit of an underdog, a bit chippy, someone who'd had to fight tooth and nail to be noticed. If someone wrote me off, it lit a fire under me, so I saw myself at a club who hadn't really won much but strived to be part of the elite, like Exeter would become. But when Bath offered me a full-time contract and some cash, all that whimsical stuff went out of the window, and I joined the most successful club of the modern era, the Manchester United of rugby, instead.

I often think about what might have happened had Geoff Wappett not spotted my potential when others didn't. I had great coaches at school, and you'd hope that someone else might have seen something special in me later down the line, but there are no guarantees in sport. If Geoff hadn't dragged me along with him, I could quite easily have slipped through the cracks, like so many decent rugby players do. And had I not got that offer from Bath and gone to uni for a couple of years instead, who knows how things might have panned out. I might have got a bad injury, I might have fallen into the typical uni life and started seeing rugby as just a bit of fun.

Of course, being presented with opportunities is one thing, but taking them is another. And I'm proud that whenever it really mattered, I took mine. Who knows what happened to the guy whose place I took at that South West trial, but I made the most of my luck that day. Then when Tom May went on study leave in the middle of that Five Nations tournament, I still had to perform to keep him out of the team. Had I not, maybe I wouldn't have gone on that tour to Australia, and I wouldn't have got any offers from Premiership clubs.

Sometimes things fall your way, sometimes they don't, and dwelling on the stuff that went wrong will send you mad eventually. People are always asking me about not playing for the Lions, injuries having scuppered my chances in 2001 and 2005. I'd have loved to go on a Lions tour, but had I done so, who knows how the rest of my career might have panned out. As such, I wouldn't change a thing about my career. You have to play the cards you're dealt.

After that Schoolboys tour to Australia, which had left me quite battered and bruised, I spent maybe a week at home before moving down to Bath, which was a bit of a shock to the system. The first guy I saw when I walked into the changing room was England captain Phil de Glanville, followed by his England team-mate Mike Catt.

There were something like 25 internationals in that Bath squad, which just doesn't happen anymore. There was Phil's club and country centre partner Jerry Guscott, plus England's Mark Regan, Ade Adebayo, Jon Callard, Victor Ubogu, Nigel Redman, Andy Long, John Mallett, Kevin Yates and Martin Haag; Scotland trio Andy Nicol, Dave Hilton and Eric Peters; and the great Wales wing Ieuan Evans. Holy shit, talk about daunting.

Rugby tended to be more hierarchical back then, and Bath's rickety old Lambridge training ground had three changing rooms – one for the big dogs, one for the small dogs, and one for the pups. The only way you could move up through the changing rooms was if someone retired and you got invited, and that kind of environment suited me. It meant I had something to prove and gave me an edge. And I soon realised that if you stood up to any rough stuff or teasing on the training ground, you got on the old pros' side pretty quickly. I managed that through my physicality, while Balsh managed it courtesy of the fact he could do things other players couldn't do and had the gift of the gab.

Not long after my arrival, Jerry Guscott, who had got me to mentor, invited me to his house, sat me down and said, 'You're not very fast, you can't pass, you can't kick. How the fuck are you going to play international rugby?' I thought that was a bit harsh, but it was the best thing he could have said to me. It made me evaluate myself to see if he was right, but it also put a bit of anger in me.

Every Thursday night, we'd play firsts versus seconds, full throttle for half an hour, which you wouldn't get away with now. Not only was it two days before an actual game, but also those playing for the seconds knew that if they could take their opposite number out, they might start that game instead.

In one of my first Thursday night games, I said to our fly-half Rich Butland, 'Just give me the ball,' before running straight over the top of Mike Catt, even standing on his head. People were shouting, 'Oh my God, he just Jonah-ed you!', referring to the time Lomu did something similar to Catty at the 1995 World Cup, and I turned to Jerry and said, 'That's how I'm gonna play international rugby ...' Over the years, I've twisted that story so that it was Jerry I ran over, not Catty, because it's neater that way.

Rugby had only been professional for a couple of years, so some of the kids coming through were proper specimens and already a physical match for some of the older players. I'd been training hard since I was 15, while some of those older guys still had an amateur mindset and avoided the gym like the plague. Don't think rugby became more professional overnight, just because players were suddenly being paid – it didn't in any shape or form. Yes, players no longer had day jobs, but really we only trained once a day with an optional gym session.

Fast forward ten years and I was the one getting shown up by kids on the training ground. These kids were training even harder than I did at school and coming into professional rugby as developed, off-the-peg athletes – huge, sculpted from hundreds of hours in the gym, quicker than me, great skills.

I didn't really drink when I was at school – I loved driving and was happy to drop people home after nights out – and, somewhat ironically, I only got into it when I turned pro.

There are a lot of hours to kill after a training session finishes at noon, and we spent a lot of long afternoons in a pub called the Chequers, while Balsh's girlfriend worked in a bar called PJ Peppers, where we were guaranteed free beer all day. Looking back, I suppose we were professional students as much as professional sportsmen, and I loved it.

Back then, you played a game, went to the bar for a few hours and had a few with opposition players, fans and sponsors, before heading to a nightclub; Po-na-na, Blue Rooms, The Swamp, The Boater, Cadillacs (RIP), the options are always good in a uni town. That happened week in, week out, whether you were playing for the firsts on a Saturday or the seconds on a Wednesday.

It doesn't sound like good practice for athletes, but in those early days of professional rugby, we were kind of just bumbling along together. I'd say we had the best of both worlds – tough rugby combined with great fun. And if you turned up for training on time the morning after the night before, veterans and coaches made a mental note that you were a proper team player.

Players tend to find more of a balance nowadays – partly because rugby has got even more attritional, partly because youngsters are more health conscious and don't feel they have to get upside down drunk to have a good time, partly because of social media and camera phones – but the social side is still a big part of the game. And it's the best part, as far as I'm concerned.

It's not as if anyone got bullied for not wanting to drink, but not many opted out. I don't think players felt they had to do it to be accepted by their team-mates or picked for the team, it was more that they enjoyed the camaraderie and sense of belonging. It was also a good way of bonding new players with old pros. Balsh, Matt 'Pezza' Perry and I went out a lot together, as did an older group including Victor and Ade, and we all mixed very well. It cost us quite a lot of money in card games, because they knew an easy mark when they saw one, but that was a price we were willing to pay.

Health, wellbeing and proper recovery weren't near the top of anyone's list of priorities – nobody even mentioned those kinds of things. At the same time, as long as you showed your face at a social, no one cared how much you drank, and it was always fairly easy to slip out of a pub once everyone else had had a few.

Steve Borthwick barely drank when he joined Bath, although I should point out that he was playing for his university, Bath seconds, and occasionally benching for the firsts. I'm not entirely sure how he got through that period, especially as he was a second-row, which is a very attritional position. We'd give him a bit of banter about it, but nothing too heavy, and if we went on an all-dayer, we might make him eat Mars Bars instead of drink beer.

Then there was my Gloucester team-mate Andy Hazell, who never really drank because he knew how bad he was at it. He became known as 'The Squirrel' because of his ability to hide his drinks. Good for him, but it had a downside for his team-mates: Hazey would document everything that happened on a night out in granular detail and tell everyone about it the next day. And when camera phones came in, he'd also have photographic evidence.

I didn't really have any rugby heroes growing up, but I did want to be like Will Carling rather than my new team-mate Jerry. Will was a similar player to me, physical and direct, and while I'm sure many an England fan shouted at their TV screen, 'Pass it to Guscott, Carling, instead of sticking it up your jumper!', he was a very handy player. Besides, Jerry only wanted the ball when he knew he could make a nice, clean break, or had enough space to put somebody else in.

Will did most of the donkey work in that centre partnership, and you can always tell one of Jerry's centre partners by the state of his face. Exhibit A is me, Exhibit B is Phil de Glanville, because you had to take a lot of hits to make Jerry look as good as he did.

I only played against Will once, in his final season for Harlequins. I said to him after the final whistle had blown, 'I've been watching you since I was eight, it's a real honour,' and he looked at me and said, 'Will you fuck off.' I reminded him of that exchange many times over the years, and now he brings it up as much as I do.

It took me until one of my final games to finally understand why Will reacted like he did that day. My centre partner was 17-year-old Ollie Thorley, who was young enough to be my son, and he played better than me. He didn't have a care in the world – it's amazing how your mind shifts as you get older – and I couldn't help thinking, *Fuck, that's annoying*.

6

FISHOMANIA

PAYNO

My first salary at Sky was £12,500, which wasn't a lot of money even in 2003, and my duties weren't much different from the time I was doing work experience. When it came to making tea, I was making good progress week by week, while no one at Sky Sports HQ in Isleworth knew their way around a photocopier better than me, not even the guy who fixed it.

The first programme I worked on as a full-time Sky employee was *FishOMania*, which was the brainchild of promoter Barry Hearn and run by his very young and up-and-coming son, Eddie. Mad as it sounds, *FishOMania* was an angling competition that had already been running on Sky for eight years (and I think is still running now!).

That year's event took place at a lake in Rotherham, and having not been told there was a dress code, I rocked up in T-shirt, shorts and flip-flops. As soon as the director saw me, he told me I was expected at the '*FishOMania* ball', (yes, you read that correctly) that evening and I needed to be smart. I had an hour to fix the problem, so found myself taking one of the company hire cars into downtown Rotherham. After driving around in circles I ended up in Asda, where I bought myself a pair of shoes, some trousers and a shirt, all for about £20. Driving back to the lake, I thought, *How did five years at Eton, four years at Edinburgh University and all that work experience lead me here, watching fishing in Rotherham in George at Asda's finest threads?* Then again, surely the only way was up. God knows what down would have looked like.

I soon found myself working on Champions League coverage, when Richard Keys and former Everton and Scotland striker Andy Gray were at the height of their powers. It was good money, because I got an additional fee, but I wasn't really into football and kept well out of the way, usually up in the gallery shuffling the sandwiches about. Keys and Gray have obviously had their headlines over the years and, from memory, there was no smoke without fire. Football dominated the agenda and the business plan at Sky, and they were allowed to build their boys club, which was filled with their devotees. I don't have a problem with that, and am not one for judging history by modern trends. It was very of its time, and a lot of people, male and female, wanted to be a part of it. But as someone whose football love was fleeting, I didn't ever try to make eye contact or want to be on the inside.

You obviously have to tread carefully when dealing with this sort of storyline, but I want to split my recollections in two. Because what is often forgotten in hindsight is how good they were at their job. And I say that as someone who kept out of the way of Richard Keys but watched what he did. And he was a very good broadcaster. He rarely used notes and never used an autocue, which is exactly how I was set up to present when the time came. The detail was all in the prep, and your links, lines and questions were all stored in your head. It certainly took a while to get comfortable with that, but I've always felt it offered real freedom with regards to bringing in stories that are unfolding around you, and developing what your guests are saying. He set the benchmark though, and we all tried to follow.

The other aspect I remember from Keys and Gray was their departure from Sky. I was still very new in the door, and I will never forget the absolute media storm as it unfolded. It led the *Ten O'Clock News*, it was on all the front pages, and the office seemed to grind to a halt for a week as it all played out in real time on Sky News. For those who don't remember, Andy Gray was caught on a hot mic making derogatory remarks about a lineswoman called Sian Massey, and from there the story just spread like wildfire. More inappropriate footage emerged from other shows, Gray was sacked, Keys resigned and then went on talk-SPORT and talked about 'dark forces' at work.

The office certainly swirled with rumours, reasons and agendas as to how and why this all unfolded, everything from clashes with other big-name presenters through to the *News of the World* scandal, but in the end they were run over by the bus they drove. People won't remember this, but several years before their exit, they both corpsed on *Monday Night Football* watching highlights of a women's football match. Uncontrollable laughter and an inability to speak.

Imagine the reaction if that happened today. The times changed, and they didn't. It was one of the first real examples of cancel culture today as we know it.

The reason I mention it is because of the label that is attached to those who present at Sky. It is a bit of a branding iron, to the extent that Keys probably left Sky 20 years ago, but on the odd occasion he pops up in the media he is referred to as 'former Sky Sports presenter'. It's one of those labels that sticks, I think, and allows the reader to judge you very quickly.

I saw this personally during the Rugby World Cup in 2023, with one of Hask's numerous features in the *Daily Mail* sidebar of shame. The papers were chasing him because of the story around him and Chloe, but, as he does, he just charged on. After a sensational lunch in the sunshine, we ended up getting quite over-excited as England beat Fiji in the quarter-finals and somehow our overzealous celebrations, complete with Hask grabbing my crotch – no, I don't know why either – ended up in the papers. And despite the fact that I'd left five years previously and GBR had taken me to far more interesting places with more interesting people, I was labelled with the infamous moniker 'former Sky Sports presenter'.

Sky Sports provokes a reaction, and a very different one to, say, the BBC. Being tagged in a way that allows the reader to make their mind up about you, place you and judge you in one pre-fix. It's exactly the same with being an Old Etonian. So to have both? I'm well and truly badged.

It's not rocket science, and most decent people don't need to be told, but in television it's a truism; be kind to people on your way up, because you'll meet the same people on your way back way down. And the rise and fall can happen very, very quickly. Progress happened rapidly for me at Sky, and within about six months I went from making tea for floor managers to having floor managers offering me a cup of coffee in the presenter's chair. I don't say that to be smart, but I can still remember the gritted teeth of one or two who'd been pretty tough as I was coming up. You don't always get it right, and live broadcasting can be incredibly intense, but I really hope that I've always been decent to those around me. It matters.

Most broadcasters back then had a very rigid hierarchy, and Sky Sports was a pyramid, with a very tight clique at the top. 'Talent', which basically meant anybody famous, would walk into a room and everyone would dance to their tune. The bowing and scraping could be uncomfortable to watch.

As with most industries, the environment was a lot tougher back then. Christ alive, there were some absolute arseholes around when I started, and there was almost an expectation that was how it had to be. As a member of the rank and file, you just tried to tread water, keep your head down and not get shot at. It was quite normal for producers and directors to dole out brutal public bollockings to underlings.

One Tuesday night, four or five of us got a going-over for not doing well enough on a Champions League show, and the following day I arrived in the gallery a couple of minutes before my call time, when the expectation was that I should have been in the gallery 15 minutes earlier. I think they do something similar in the military. The director gave me a proper coating, rang the head of the production runners, said I wasn't taking it seriously and that he wanted me gone. That could have been the end of my career in broadcasting – boom, over in a flash – but, mercifully, Martin Turner stepped in and said, 'No, he's already proved himself, he's staying.' One of those sliding-doors moments. I actually saw the same director, back in at Sky, 20-something years later while presenting another Lions tour. We had a very civil chat, a few compliments here and there, a check-in on how things had changed over the years. And no mention of the fact that he almost cut my dreams dead in one call. But I think we both knew.

On another occasion in my early days, I was editing a Saturday Premiership rugby match into the highlights show, which I'd then put on to two tapes and take down to transmission. They'd then roll out those highlights throughout the weekend, to fill the gaps in the channels. I was desperate to get to a party in Oxford that evening, so really rushed things. And less than a minute after I'd handed the tapes to the relevant bloke in transmission and filled in the paperwork, I was in my banger of a car, on my way.

I left this party at about two in the morning, and when I got back to my car, which was my bed for the night, I had about 15 missed calls and seven voicemails. It turned out I'd taken the wrong tape out of the machine and put it in the wrong box before handing it to transmission. So at 9 o'clock, when people were expecting to see the rugby they'd missed that afternoon, they actually got the last third of some random basketball match. Transmission had phoned the executive producer, who'd phoned the sub-producer, and both of them had phoned me – repeatedly, and with increasing levels of anger.

I wish I'd kept those voicemails, because they would have been a window into a long-forgotten world. And I'm not sure I'd have ever had to work again – the payout would have been fantastic. They were spectacularly inappropriate by modern standards – 'You fucked up big time! You're incompetent! How fucking dare you! I've had to cancel my plans and drive an hour to Isleworth to sort your shit out! Don't bother coming into the office on Monday! You'll never fucking work for Sky again!' – and I listened to them with my head in my hands, thinking, *You got to where you wanted to be in life, and now you've managed to cock it up over the simplest of jobs.*

I wrote grovelling emails the following day, and to my relief, their response was, 'Don't worry about it, get back in on Monday and tidy your mess up.' That was usually how it was back then: you ballsed up, the bosses unloaded on you with furious anger, you said sorry, they accepted your apology, and everyone carried on as if nothing had happened.

It was a world away from how most workplaces operate nowadays. I have a tech business which employs 20 people, and if I spoke to any of them the way some of my bosses spoke to me, I'd end up in a tribunal and I'd lose. And while I'd never advocate bosses swearing at their staff, I do sometimes wonder if the baby has been thrown out with the bathwater.

Hask speaks about the old-school environment he came through at Wasps, and how much it benefited him. If he wasn't performing as he should have, he'd be told. And because the criticism was so honest and cut so deep, he spent a lot of time analysing his performances and striving to get better. Tins' experience in rugby was much the same, and that's why the conversations we have now are so frank. We'll say when something wasn't good enough and we'll admit when we've cocked up. Well, Tins and I will anyway.

Broadcasting isn't sport, but Sky Sports at that time was a high-performance machine, in full challenger mode to its opposition, and employees either accepted the inevitable bollockings that came their way, or they fell off the ride. I saw lots of workmates come and go, but I just about managed to cling on, despite my early career being littered with disasters. And far from looking back on those times and thinking, *I never should have had to put up with that*, I remember them with fondness. I'm proud of my battle scars and I'm grateful to the people who inflicted them on me, because they made me better at my job. In fact, I've remained friends with many of them to this day.

7

AMAZED TO BE PLAYING RUGBY

TINS

My first game for Bath was for the seconds against Gloucester. We won by 40-odd points, although it wasn't really a fair contest because we had about 12 internationals in our side. My team-mates included Balsh, Ieuan Evans, Ade Adebayo, Andy Nicol, Victor Ubogu, Eric Peters, Dave Hilton, Andy Long, Wales back-row Nathan Thomas and Argentina lock Germán Llanes.

I spent most of that game trailing Ieuan, who no one could tackle, and ended up scoring two tries from just being on his shoulder to beat the full-back. And as mad (and unfair) as it was to have so many quality operators turning out for the seconds, I learned so much from playing and training with men who had been there and done it. I think that's why the likes of Balsh, Pez (Eric Peters), Longy and myself got called up by England so early in our careers, and it's a shame that youngsters today miss out on that experience.

I don't remember much about my first-team debut, except that it was against Bristol on my 19th birthday – 18 October

1997 – I came on as a replacement for Pezza and we thumped them. Oh, and Kevin Yates did a wonderful job on me in the pub afterwards, buying me a drink consisting of every white spirit in a pint glass – and pork scratchings. I made the rookie mistake of saying it didn't taste too bad after I had finished it, so he went and bought me another one, which was the end of me. I woke up on top of a car, but fortunately one of the boys was walking past at the time and managed to get me home.

A couple of months later, I made my first start for the first team, which didn't go well. We got pummelled by Saracens at Vicarage Road, and that 50–23 defeat is remembered as one of the worst in Bath's history. It was the first time any team had put 50 points on Bath since the introduction of league rugby in England, and while it was great in theory to share a pitch with Sarries' World Cup winners Francois Pienaar and Michael Lynagh, the reality was rather different.

Mum and Dad came to every single game I played, whether it was for the firsts or seconds, for about three years. They'd finish work before jumping in the car and travelling down from Yorkshire to Bath for some inconsequential second team game, drive straight back afterwards, get home at some ungodly hour, then go to work the next morning.

Mum would bring a big cooler box full of ready meals, which would last me, Mearsy and Balsh for a month. But while that was amazing commitment on their part, and I really did appreciate the support and the grub, I did say to them eventually, 'You don't have to burden yourselves, you'll end up killing yourselves.' Dad, in typically blunt fashion, replied, 'You never know when it's going to end ...'

That didn't exactly feel like a vote of confidence, but it was only really in the 2001–02 season that I started to feel comfortable and they realised there might be plenty more mileage in my career and stopped coming to every game. It didn't stop Dad saying he was a better centre than me, and he still says that to this day. When I ask him to show me his CV and point out that playing against Headingley isn't quite in the same league as winning a World Cup, he goes quiet, but I think he really loved living out the career he never had through me.

In my first couple of seasons, our centre partnership was very mix and match. Jerry Guscott was a shoo-in when fit, although he had a lot of injury problems and retired after the 1999 World Cup. I played with him a few times, but when he was on the sidelines, there were a variety of combinations made up of me, Pezza, Catty and Phil. My first long-running midfield partnership was with Ireland centre Kevin Maggs, which lasted three or four years.

I never forgot how lucky I was to have come of age just after rugby turned professional, and I spent my early years at Bath amazed to be playing rugby for a living. However, I barely made any money for the first four or five years of my career. My first wage was £10k, which wasn't much even in 1997. My dad, being a bank manager, still insisted I start paying into a pension, which made living even leaner, we often chose not to heat the house, so there were duvets all over the lounge. It meant we had more money for fun, although we could always decamp to PJ Peppers, where we were assured of warmth and free beer.

We were also paid a £500 match fee for every first-team game, and you could triple your pay packet for the month if you played your cards right. I'd fight tooth and nail to win a place and numerous times sat on the bench with injuries, broken ribs and a busted AC joint. Fortunately, I didn't get on!

There was a big gap between guys like me, who joined Bath after rugby had turned pro, and those superstars who played in the amateur era. Some of those guys were earning between £150k and £200k, which is a good wage for a rugby player almost 30 years later, the problem being that club owners lost millions of pounds in the first couple of seasons.

Players understandably demanded decent wages, especially those who already had well-paid jobs, and owners will say they didn't really have much choice but to pay up. Unfortunately, they were doing their calculations on the hoof, got the balance all wrong, and English rugby has been on the back foot ever since.

My wage more than doubled for my second season, before the salary cap was introduced in 1999, Richmond and London Scottish having gone into administration. Balsh's and my careers were sort of tracking together, with him getting slightly more games for the firsts than myself and when he went back in for a meeting with Andy Robinson and came out with a raise, I thought I was in for the same treatment. Unfortunately, I got told I was getting reduced from £22.5k to £20k. Even worse, they also removed the contract clause that said anyone who played for England immediately jumped to £60k, which meant I was an England player on £20k for a couple of seasons.

Bath would tell me I should be on more money, but they didn't want to give me anything like non-internationals playing for other clubs were getting (rugby is a small world, so you often heard what other players were earning on the grapevine, even if it was just a ballpark figure). I was still on between £40k and £50k when we won the World Cup in 2003, although fans assumed we were all earning hundreds of thousands, and my Bath salary started to make less and less sense.

The timing was key. I was 26, probably in my athletic prime, and you never know how long you've got left in the game. I was a World Cup winner, a Grand Slam winner, had won 35 caps for England. I'd been players' player of the year and fans' player of the year, and this was the first time I'd had the opportunity to earn close to my actual worth, rather than what Bath told me my worth was.

Money was the main reason I finally left, but Bath weren't doing great on the pitch either. We'd lost something like 15 internationals in a couple of years and replaced them with loads of youngsters, the result being that we very nearly got relegated in 2002–03. The club did invest that summer, and we reached the Premiership final in 2003–04, but it didn't feel quite the same. Not that we'd had much success with all those internationals in the team.

It's a nice silver lining that most of the stuff I won was for England, but I wish I'd had more success at club level. International rugby is the cherry on top, but club rugby is a player's bread and butter. Unfortunately, it never really clicked during my time at Bath. We did win the Heineken Cup in 1998, but I wasn't involved in any of the games (I watched the final at home in Yorkshire with my mum and dad, before jumping in my car and driving down to Bath for the celebrations), and Bath didn't land another trophy until winning the Premiership title in 2024–25.

We reached the Premiership final in 2003–04 against Wasps, but despite having most of the ball, and their hooker Trevor Leota being so off target that we were calling backs moves off his line-out throws, we couldn't deal with their blitz defence and lost 10–6.

I got a decent uplift after the World Cup, before I had a tough year with injuries in 2003–04. I was back fit the following season, when my contract was up for renewal, so I said to them, 'Look, I love Bath. I don't want to go to another club, or use other clubs as leverage, but you've had me cheap for years. I just want you to be fair and pay me what I deserve.' I told them I'd happily sign on the spot for £150k, and they told me they couldn't afford it and offered me £20k less.

It had nothing to do with arrogance or greed, it was about wanting to feel valued, to have control, rather than Bath always having the upper hand. And the longer Bath dragged their feet, the more annoyed I got. I'd been there for eight years, and I felt they were playing on my loyalty. I was convinced they were deliberately running down time, so I'd miss the chance of joining another club before the start of the next season. But they didn't understand that while I'm generally an easy-going bloke, I'm only flexible to a certain point, and just when people think I'm about to break, I'll snap back the other way.

I confided in our Aussie fly-half Chris Malone, who was adamant that I should stay, and he was also telling Jack Rowell, who was in charge of contracts, that the club needed me, but they wouldn't budge. And when they still hadn't got any closer to £150k by January 2005, after four months of meetings, I thought, *Fuck it, it's not worth it*, and started speaking to other clubs.

Saracens and Sale both made decent offers, but Gloucester also wanted to sign me, and I decided to join them instead. Soon after, Jack came to me and said, 'We'd better get this contract sorted,' before offering me what I'd asked for. But I had to tell him that they'd left it too late and I'd agreed to sign for Gloucester instead, and they also had budgets and strategies to organise.

Gloucester offered less than Sarries and Sale, but a move there made more sense from a rugby and personal perspective. I was going out with Zara, and moving to Sarries or Sale would have made our situation much harder, not least because she had 12 or 13 horses to look after. So it was a good job really that Gloucester were even interested.

When he heard I'd signed, Jerry contacted me and said, 'Please don't tell the public you're going for an extra £10k, say it's a significant pay rise.' I told him that it *was* a significant pay rise! And it was what I deserved to be paid.

People in Bath were upset, but the game had been pro for ten years by then, and the idea that players shouldn't move to local rivals was already outdated. Steve Ojomoh moved from Bath to Gloucester shortly after my arrival at the Rec, while Rob Fidler went the other way in 2003, so while it was still frowned upon by some, I didn't get the flak I might have done a few years earlier.

Bath had an online forum, where fans went to discuss all things to do with the club, and I had a look to see what they were saying about me. Some people understood why I'd made the decision to leave, some didn't and were disappointed in me, so I went on there and tried to explain my decision. Without mentioning names, I told them what centres who weren't even in the England set-up were being paid at other clubs (as much as £200k, in case you were wondering), I told them my wage history at Bath, and I explained that if I had been leaving just for cash, I'd have gone somewhere else rather than Gloucester.

Some people were sympathetic, others argued that paying me however much more would prevent Bath from signing someone else they needed. To that point, I could only answer, 'That's not really my problem.'

8

I MIGHT BECOME A BROADCASTER

PAYNO

As well as football, I worked on a lot of tennis over-nights, which tested a man's soul, but a few months after I joined, Sky won the rights for the Heineken Cup, and suddenly they needed a lot more people in the rugby department.

Once again, I was in the right place at the right time – the luck part again – but I was also playing the long game. The producers of the Champions League coverage would often give production runners screen tests, and I'd watched two or three of my colleagues do one and thought, *I'm curious to try that*.

The trouble for those who made a song and a dance about wanting to be on screen was that they then couldn't get into a specific department, which is where your career would really progress, because everyone knew that all they wanted to do was present. I made sure not to overplay my hand and was duly invited to join the rugby team as a junior production assistant.

My presenting curiosity on hold, I remained a dogsbody, although I was at least getting to do a bit of editing and more match-day work and a bit of filming out and about. One of my first gigs was to interview Martin Johnson for *The Rugby Club*, our magazine show, after he got home from leading England to World Cup glory. Talk about straight off the top diving board. Johnno never much liked the media, and he was being pulled in every direction that day, but he was decent enough to answer my questions, albeit with an air of 'I really don't have time for this.'

His England and Leicester team-mate Neil Back was hovering over my shoulder, almost like his bodyguard, and after my fourth or fifth question, he jumped in with, 'Got what you wanted? Can he go now?' 'Yep,' I replied, 'thanks very much indeed …' I had loads more questions, but I was very easily dissuaded as a green 23-year-old. Plus, you try telling both of them what you really think …

Weirdly, later that night I'd been given two tickets to the premiere of *The Lord of the Rings* in London, and my brother and I wandered up the red carpet, milking the opportunity. But things got a little odd when we reached our seats, because Neil Back was in the seat next to me. He looked at me with no little disappointment and whispered, 'How the hell have you got here?' I felt a bit sorry for him: there he was, enjoying yet another perk for winning the World Cup, and some chimp junior production assistant was riding up front in his moment of glory.

Those early days were just learning lessons in fast forward. And one of the most important came after one of the best games I've ever worked on. The classic Heineken Cup semi-final between Munster and Wasps at the old Lansdowne Road in 2004 is still a game for the ages, when Trevor Leota's last-gasp try secured victory for the reigning Premiership champions. Roy Keane was in the crowd, the sun shone, the match swung this way and that, and off the back of it the Sky crew got extremely drunk in Dublin that evening and ended up running into the Wasps team in a nightclub.

One member of Sky's talent was last seen heading back to the hotel with one of the players' sisters – in a horse-drawn carriage – and I'll never forget saying hello to Trevor Leota, who was carrying about 16 pints, and him replying, 'Out of the way, cunt.' (I reminded him about it recently, and he laughed heartily before offering a grovelling apology).

Later that night, I attempted to congratulate Trevor's fellow front-rower Will Green on his performance (he was upside down drunk, so had no idea what I was going on about), and a Sky colleague took me aside and said, 'Look, you've got to learn this really quickly: they are the rugby players, we are the broadcasters. We aren't friends, and there's a line you don't cross.'

He was absolutely right. I'd thought that mixing with those blokes, in the playground of the gods, was a perk of the job. But to be able to tell the stories properly we needed distance, and cultivating friendships makes that more difficult.

The same went for tittle-tattle, as one of my good friends learned to his cost. One morning, we were in the office early, chewing the fat over a coffee. We both received an email saying that a famous sportsman was going to be outed as gay by one of the red tops later that day. We speculated and guessed, and I then went off to edit a feature for *The Rugby Club*. But my friend sent the email on to a couple of his mates, with his own thoughts on who the sportsman was, and by the time I'd finished editing at midday, my friend had been hauled in by Sky's lawyers. His forwarded email, with his signature on the bottom, had spread like wildfire and leaked onto chatrooms and message boards, the sportsman's agent was threatening to sue, the sportsman himself had been pulled out of training and was, unsurprisingly, up in arms, and my friend was absolutely shitting himself.

This was before social media as we know it now, so it was probably my first experience of something going viral on the internet. And it fascinated me that while I'd been quietly working away in a dark editing suite for a couple of hours, my friend had set fire to a forest and was watching it burn. There were apologies and things eventually got cleared up, but it was a lesson I've never forgotten.

If I ever hear, 'Oh my God, you'll never guess what I heard' I'll always say, 'Is this something I need to know?' Unless I'm meant to and am allowed to talk about it, I don't want to be privy to that information. More importantly, I can never remember what I am and am not allowed to talk about, so not knowing just makes life easier.

One Friday evening, I was in the office logging some match footage when Martin said, 'Damn, I haven't got a reporter for the game tomorrow. Alex, what are you down to do?' I told him I was meant to be inputting stats for the game at Twickenham, and he replied, 'Don't worry about that, you're going to be our reporter. Let's see how you get on …'

I had done a couple of short, recorded interviews by then, and I assume Martin thought I'd done all right, but I was 24, I looked about 12, I'd never received any broadcasting training, or done any acting or public speaking, and I didn't have an enormous amount of confidence. I did, however, have a real desire to give it a go.

Having turned up at 9 a.m., I was due on air by 10.30. And when someone put a microphone in my hand, it felt more like a loaded gun. That day at Twickenham was a bit like walking along a precipice, knowing that if I put one foot wrong, or if there was a strong gust, everything I was aiming for would be over.

It was the annual fixture between the Army and the Navy at a sold-out Twickenham – not exactly a World Cup final, although it felt like that to me – and on the final whistle, I ran onto the pitch with a cameraman to grab an instant reaction. My very first live interview victim was Scotland and Army prop Mattie Stewart, who probably wondered who the hell the overly excited kid sticking a mic in his face was, but I just about got some words out and managed to do the job. But wow, it lit a spark – the extraordinary high of live television was utterly intoxicating, and I wanted more.

9

UNBREAKABLE

PAYNO

During my time at Sky, a couple of ex-professional players left their professionalism on the pitch and put the 'tour' into 'tourist'. The first time I worked with one famous former player, we were meant to pick him up from his hotel in the south of France, en route from Clermont to Toulouse. But we soon discovered that he hadn't checked in, and we eventually tracked him down at about 10 a.m., climbing out of a bush in his dinner suit. 'Give us a couple of minutes,' he said, 'I'll just grab my things and be right with you ...' He changed on the bus and was on air a couple of hours later, looking bright-eyed and bushy tailed.

We were on tour together a couple of years later, and one Sunday night when I was already in bed, he popped through a little text saying 'Shall we have a little wander into town?' Before the tour I'd read a book called *The Yes Man*, where the writer says yes to everything, and I'd made a pact with myself to do similar on tour. So I got up, got dressed, headed out for a cracker and was back in before the sun came up a few hours later. As for my famous friend, he wasn't seen again until the Thursday morning. They found him having a snooze in the corner of a casino lift; apparently he'd been going up and down for hours.

I saw plenty of guests come and go during my time at Sky, proof that punditry is an even more precarious trade than presenting. Not all players achieve enough in the game to get the call in the first place, and their window of opportunity can be very small. The bright lights are also not for everyone – I've been in the studio with players who've got stuck in the headlights and only given one-word answers, players who've sweated up a storm, players who've asked me what they should be talking about and players who've found television far worse than playing.

During the recent Lions tour, I had to deliver an opening monologue at the top of the show that was about three minutes long. It involved a match caption to identify the game, location shots to show where the match was taking place, talking through the Lions' team selection, welcoming each of our guests in both studio and pitchside in Australia, and then throwing to head coach Andy Farrell who was with our reporter. It requires a bit of prep and holding a fair bit of information in your head before trying to deliver it with plenty of energy, without stumbling or repetition. After I had to deliver the intro for one of the warm-up matches, Anthony Watson said, 'I simply don't know how you do that,' and Sam Warburton added, 'And that's why you're the presenter and I will always be the pundit.'

I actually think Sam would make a fantastic presenter, but the truth is it's only words, and if you do it for long enough you find a way to (hopefully) get it right more often than not. The far more impressive thing will forever be stepping across the whitewash and playing a sport that tests every fibre of your being, and doing so in front of tens of thousands in the stands and millions watching on television. But when those heroes step into our environment and raise an eyebrow of appreciation, it reminds me that live TV definitely has a pressure valve attached to it.

But as far as the media is concerned, for a year or two after you retire from playing, you're seen as a fresh, exciting face with your finger on the pulse of the current game. There is, however, a constant stream of shiny new opinions every season. For example, 2025 saw the retirement of Harlequins and England legend Danny Care, who is moving into punditry. It will mean one or two of the older guard get less work. It's brutal, although not much different to professional sport.

Which leads me to England's 2003 World Cup-winning team. I found the recent documentary about those boys, *Unbreakable: England 2003*, quite jaw-dropping and very sad. When you think of how their success captured the imagination of the nation, and how famous they once were, the fact that quite a few of them seem to have fallen through the cracks is difficult to compute.

Phil Vickery, one of the game's great men, was recently declared bankrupt and joined the concussion lawsuit; Steve Thompson was diagnosed with early-onset dementia in 2020 and can't remember anything about winning the World Cup; Ben Cohen sold his winner's medal to make ends meet during the Covid pandemic; Jonny Wilkinson, the biggest hero of all, has spoken at length about his own struggles; the unbreakable Lawrence Dallaglio has had his financial difficulties plastered all over the media. Some will no doubt say, 'People from all walks of life struggle, why do those guys think they're special in some way?' But I don't think they're claiming to be special, I think they're talking about their various issues to show that they can happen to anyone, however successful one's life appears to be.

I interviewed most of that squad when they were at the peak of their powers and it's fairly heartbreaking to see where some of them are now. Major sportspeople breathe rarefied air, and those players were alpha males doing extraordinary things with millions watching. That World Cup win was a magical moment in English sport, and some of the players would have spent much of their lives since searching for something that might replicate that feeling, while knowing deep down that nothing would ever come close.

As much as I love the game and the people who play it, I'm increasingly of the opinion that rugby players are an odd bunch. They train relentlessly, asking things of their body and mind that very few people could comprehend, all so they can beat the shit out of other people and have the shit beaten out of them on a weekend. Do that for 10 to 15 years, and you become a very particular kind of person, and suddenly you have to give that life up and do something 'normal'. Some chased dreams that never materialised, some were led down the garden path business-wise, some will need care for the rest of their lives and regret ever playing rugby.

They've chosen to speak out because people still remember and adore them, and Vicks explained it better than me: 'I'm Phil Vickery – "Raging Bull", MBE, England captain, World Cup winner, European Cup winner – but actually I've fucking struggled. If [saying that] helps somebody, brilliant.'

Vicks has been on the pod a couple of times, once with Ben Cohen, and it was really sad to hear them say that they wouldn't play rugby if they had their time again. I don't know what the answer is really, but it doesn't reflect very well on the game in this country that it hasn't been able to look after the best team it has ever produced, and one of the best teams in the game's history. Very few from that team have an active involvement in the coaching or running of the game at the elite level in this country. What an extraordinary waste of the most valuable rugby IP.

Several World Cup winners have launched Champions 2003, which began as a network of support and benevolence for those members of the squad in need and soon grew into a charity which seeks to help any former professional player struggling in retirement. Tins is always missing calls and pods because he's knee deep in Champions 2003 meetings – forever the team man, even if he does have his head in his hands a lot of the time.

I still think rugby is a game that gives most people who play it more than it takes, but at the elite level, it remains a nominally professional endeavour run in a very amateur way. It's had a desperately difficult last 10 to 15 years, what with clubs struggling – and in some cases failing – to stay afloat, administrators making disastrously short-sighted decisions regarding broadcasting, which has made the game less visible, and constant negative headlines over brain injuries and players still not being looked after properly, neither financially nor physically.

It's a great frustration of mine that rugby is still unable to set players up for life, and that most players will retire in their early 30s with a knee facing the wrong way, a shoulder that pops out every time they do front crawl, a big mortgage, an expensive car, and a partner who is accustomed to a certain lifestyle. But I genuinely hope and believe that the game will find a way back to positivity, and that the boys of 2003 might be the example that forces change.

HASK

The England team of 2003 … well, they did a rather good thing, didn't they? Won the actual World Cup, beat the Aussies in their own backyard, became instant heroes. You'd think, after such heroics, they'd be looked after like national treasures. Polished, dusted, stuck in a glass cabinet next to the Crown Jewels. Alas, rugby doesn't quite work like that.

Each player's journey was different: some didn't even make the squad for the final, others played every minute, and everyone had their lives turned upside down. Some of the boys maximised it, went on to media careers, coaching, motivational speaking. Others … well, the documentary *Unbreakable: England 2003* showed just how badly some have struggled. Watching it was painful – less *Band of*

Brothers, more like an episode of *Can't Pay? We'll Take It Away!*

Now, if the England football team won the World Cup, those lads could live forever on after-dinner speeches, selling signed boots on eBay and pointing at a framed shirt behind them on Zoom calls. They'd never have to lift a finger again. But rugby? Nowhere near as big. Your audience shrinks the moment the final whistle goes. And here's the cold truth: no matter what you've achieved, you can't just swan about expecting people to shower you with cash. That goes for soldiers who've fought for their country, and it goes for sportsmen who've lifted trophies. You've still got to earn your crust.

I learned that lesson early. Yes, I won a Heineken Cup, a Premiership title and a Grand Slam. Gorgeous moments, lovely medals. But you can't bask in that forever, can you? There's always another tournament, another winner, another fresh-faced lad on a billboard with his shirt off. People stop caring quicker than you can say 'remember my open-top bus parade?' Before you know it, you're yesterday's chip paper.

And I do get why some people say, 'They had their day, they got the medals, the Downing Street reception why should they get special treatment now? Just get a job like the rest of us.' Fair point. But, and it's a big but, the players should've been encouraged to plan ahead while they were still on the pitch. Ironically, some of that 2003 squad gave me grief for prepping for life after rugby. 'Oh Haskell, stop doing media, focus on rugby!' Cut to 20 years later and perhaps it was not such a silly thing to have done.

The truth is, if you took any random group of workmates from 20 years ago – teachers, plumbers, builders, fluffers (don't ask), whatever – you'd see the same spread: some doing brilliantly, some barely hanging on, some blissfully happy, some in a bad way. That's just life. But because the 2003 team moved millions of people, there's this unspoken assumption rugby would have checked in occasionally. A phone call. A WhatsApp group. Something more than silence.

Problem is, that generation weren't exactly into sharing feelings. They were the ultimate alpha males: play hard, drink hard, never cry unless it's over a spilt pint. Now, in their fifties, it's even less likely they'll pipe up and say, 'Actually lads, I'm struggling here.'

Contrast that with my lot. When Chloe and I separated, the phone didn't stop ringing. When my dad died, old team-mates were all over me, checking in. Which is lovely. But it makes you wonder: if rugby can't even look after its greatest heroes, the men who won the bloody World Cup, then what hope is there for the rank and file?

TINS

Maybe I'd think differently if I had suffered permanent brain damage from rugby – my memory is pretty good, and I've had checks on my brain and nothing has shown up so far – but when it comes to that particular topic, I'm kind of on the other side of the debate than some of my old team-mates.

I think the game punishes itself too much, and there are a lot of elements to early-onset dementia. If you looked at how I played the game, you'd think I'd be a prime candidate for brain injury. I was physical, a hard, straight-running centre, and God knows how many tackles I made during my career. That suggests there are genetic factors, as well as how cleanly or not players live their lives away from the game.

I've heard former team-mates say they wished they'd never picked up a rugby ball, which makes me quite sad. Yes, the game can do more to help players when they transition out of the game, but former players suing (almost 800 have joined a concussion lawsuit against the sport's authorities, according to recent reports) is taking money from the sport, which could go into looking after players better, including regular brain scans and benevolent funds.

It should never be forgotten that while playing rugby comes with risks, it is a choice, and we shouldn't be going down the road of telling people what they can and can't do. And if we start messing around with the game too much, in terms of toning down the physicality, you're going to make it less attractive to the public.

Big hits and collisions are what most people want the sport to be about, partly because they know they couldn't do that themselves. Talk to an NFL player about rugby and one of the first things he'll say is, 'I'd never want to do anything like that without pads and helmets.' And rugby is far too apologetic about its incredible physicality, when it should be celebrated.

Maybe the amateur and pro games are getting confused in people's minds because they're run by the same unions.

The amateur game has got to be fun and safe, while also being competitive, but it should be emphasised that it's not the same as elite rugby. Elite rugby is about hard, bloody-nosed competition, with the best athletes going at it hammer and tongs for 80 minutes, and the team that wants it most winning.

People haven't gone after rugby league in the same way, and I wonder if that's a bit of a class thing. A lot of public schools play union, and the parents get involved way more than in the state sector, and it's not always to the benefit of the sport. But rugby in schools shouldn't be mimicking what happens at Twickenham on a Saturday anyway – it should be made clear that they're two completely different things.

The second Test between the Lions and Australia in 2025 was a great example of the best that rugby can offer. The Aussies flew out of the traps, there was niggle and there was immense physicality. Maro Itoje and Will Skelton really went at each other, but after the final whistle, Skelton said to Maro, 'Sorry, bro, I've got to do this for my country …' They're mates off the field, they played together at Saracens, but for those 80 minutes, they were enemies. That's a skillset in itself, and something that people should be amazed by, but instead of saying, 'That's the power of rugby,' the sport is reluctant to highlight that kind of story because it touches on the rougher side of the game.

We decided to set up Champions 2003 after the 20-year anniversary reunion. Benny Cohen put a video on our group chat, saying we should do something, and six of us took it up from there – Benny, me, Ben Kay, Matt Dawson, Phil Vickery and Andy Gomarsall. The initial aim was to focus on the issues some of the World Cup winners had – brain injuries, mental health struggles, financial struggles, just people trying to work out life after rugby.

Some of those 2003 guys have done really well outside of the game, but some have had a bit of a rough time of things. And we didn't want what happened to England's 1966 Football World Cup winners – many of whom felt the need to sell their medals and shirts – to happen to our group (although Benny Cohen recently revealed on talkSPORT that he'd sold his 2003 medal to make ends meet during Covid, which made fellow guest Phil Vickery cry).

People assume that 2003 side is constantly meeting up, but in that respect, sport is no different from any other job. People retire at different times, have kids, fall into other work, find new friends, meet new partners, move abroad, and before you know it, the group has grown so far apart that that you can't imagine ever getting back together.

Having said that, one of the most special things about rugby is the camaraderie. I played for two clubs over 17 years and whenever I see an old team-mate, regardless of when I last saw them, it's like we've never been apart. Only the other day, I bumped into my old Bath and England team-mate Michael Lipman in Australia, and we just picked up from where we left off. And it's not much different with people I played against. I also met the great Australian centre Timmy Horan recently and the subject of the time I flattened him playing for Bath against Saracens back in the day definitely came up.

Did the boys of 2003 function perfectly all the time? No, but we did very well on a rugby field, and it's nice to remind ourselves of that once in a while. Maybe the guys who wished they'd never picked up a rugby ball might even change their minds. On a more basic level, it's good to just check up on old mates, to see how they're doing and if they might need a bit of a helping hand.

10

DON'T FUCK IT UP, MATE

PAYNO

In September 2004, I was given the official title of junior reporter, and one of my jobs was to film a round-up of the Championship games on a show called *The Rugby Club*.

I was diabolical – looked about 15, sounded about 12 – and I can't really tell you how I survived, except to say that they must have seen something that they could work with. And they had me doing some amazing stuff, including learning to goal kick with Wales's Neil Jenkins, learning to tackle with France's Sébastien Chabal, a fitness session with London Scottish (which made me puke), and a sidestepping clinic with England's Jason Robinson.

There have been few better steppers in the game than Jason, so I didn't really expect to lay a glove on him. But having set things up for the cameras – a load of kids forming a narrow channel, Jason at one end, me at the other, in full Sale kit, scrumcap and gumshield – and explained what we needed Jason to do, namely run towards me while explaining what he was thinking and what his body was doing, I nailed him, knocking over a couple of kids in the process.

Jason is a great guy, but even nice-guy sportsmen don't like people taking liberties. He looked straight at the camera and said, 'I had no idea we were taking it that seriously. Now I'm going to show the smart arse.' From that point on, it was like trying to catch Scotch mist, and I could tell he relished tying me in knots. However, I can tell my grandchildren that I once tackled the great Jason Robinson, which many players failed to do over the years.

One of the first reports I ever did, in March 2005, was from an England Under-21s training camp at Franklin's Gardens, before a Six Nations game against Scotland. I was watching a scrummaging session, and just as it looked as though they were about to finish, I suggested to my cameraman that we head into the stadium to get set up for my interviews. I was getting the tripod legs out of the car when the team coach Pete Drewett went haring past, and when I said, 'Christ, you're in a hurry,' he replied, 'Yeah, there's been a terrible accident …' It gives me goosebumps just thinking about it now.

Next thing I knew, ambulances were screeching into the carpark, players were filing past looking haunted, and we finally got the news that young Leicester prop Matt Hampson had suffered a serious injury. That was our cue to pack up our things and make ourselves scarce.

The following day, I had to do a report from Stoke Mandeville Hospital, where 'Hambo' was having a surgery on his spine. I feel quite uncomfortable about that now, but I suppose that's the role of a news reporter. I brought along a get well soon card from all at Sky Rugby (which seems odd in hindsight – you tell someone with the sniffles to get well soon, not someone who has just suffered a catastrophic spinal injury), but sadly the news wasn't good. Hambo spent 18 months in Stoke Mandeville and remains paralysed from the neck down.

However, as tragic as Hambo's story is, he's admitted that the accident probably made him a better person than he otherwise would have been. He's a truly remarkable bloke, and what he's achieved since that terrible day in Northampton is probably a lot bigger than he would have achieved as a rugby player. The Matt Hampson Foundation supports young people seriously injured through sport and has raised a lot of awareness and money over the years. And perhaps just as importantly, Hambo has shown that you can still have a very fulfilling life after suffering a profoundly life-changing injury.

Hambo has played quite a big part in the lives of me, Hask and Tins. Hask was on the training ground with Hambo that fateful day, I was there as a reporter, and Tins is heavily involved with the Matt Hampson Foundation, serving as patron and raising large sums of money from his annual golf day. In addition, a chunk of cash from our Blackeye Rugby Fund goes to the Matt Hampson Foundation every year.

Every time we meet is a treat. I still host dinners for his charity, we've interviewed him for the podcast and he's a bloody funny guest. We also bumped into him at the 2023 Rugby World Cup in France where he was at the centre of it all. He was very pissed – not quite doing donuts in his wheelchair, but not far off.

I wouldn't claim to be incredibly close to Hambo, but I have enormous respect for him. I've chatted to lots of people who have done extraordinary things down the years, but what he's done tops the lot in terms of the hand he's been dealt and how he's played it. When he could have spent the rest of his life wallowing in self-pity, he chose instead to do incredible work for people less fortunate than him.

Around the time of Hambo's accident, Martin informed me that Graham Simmons, one of the best sports reporters of his generation and a man I learned so much from, didn't want to do the entire Lions tour, because of family commitments, and was only going to come down to New Zealand for the Test matches. Will Chignell, who would have filled in for Graham, had a family emergency, so they were sending me – six months into the job – down instead, for the whole 11 weeks of the Lions tour. It was, to put it mildly, a rapid rise through the ranks. It wouldn't happen now. It shouldn't have happened then.

A few months later – less than a year since being made a junior reporter, and four years since blowing a student loan on getting myself to a Lions tour in Australia – I was flying business-class to report on a Lions tour in New Zealand. And I was excited beyond belief. But as time went on, excitement turned to fear, as it dawned on me that I didn't know what I was meant to be doing. I barely slept for days before the Lions' first game, against Bay of Plenty in Rotorua.

My first task was a 90-second live from pitchside to the studio, with Stuart Barnes alongside. It was very basic stuff – 'Hello and welcome to Rotorua. Stuart, who needs to play well? What would be a good outcome for the Lions? Back to you in the studio …' – but I cannot tell you how terrified I was. I can still remember being awake in the middle of the night mulling through the significance, the number of people who'd be watching, the job pressure. However, I'd rehearsed the segment over and over and managed to bumble my way through it. Barnesy, who was a hard taskmaster with very high standards, would probably have said that I shouldn't have been anywhere near New Zealand, although, to be fair to him, he was supportive enough.

That was a rough 11 weeks for the Lions, starting with a tour-ending injury to Lawrence Dallaglio in that very first game. I had to interview him the next day, post-surgery, and I brought him the newspapers and some wine gums. My first question was, 'Did you know immediately it was bad?' To which he answered, 'Well, my foot was on the wrong way round, so I knew it wasn't great.' Frost v Nixon it wasn't.

With his jaw-jutting defiance gone, the tour drifted from bad to worse to desperate, all to a backdrop of incessant Kiwi rain. After skipper Brian O'Driscoll dislocated his shoulder less than two minutes into the first Test, caused by the infamous double tackle of Tana Umaga and Keven Mealamu, it became nothing short of a rabble. And for the first time, I found myself not really enjoying any of it.

Former Labour Party attack dog Alastair Campbell was the Lions' press officer, and I fell victim to his devious political machinations before the game against Otago in Dunedin. Just as a press conference was about to kick off, he took me aside and said, 'Could you possibly ask [assistant coach] Ian McGeechan what the Lions have been doing to win hearts and minds in New Zealand?'

Of course, I did exactly as he suggested, Geech trotted out a seemingly rehearsed answer about spreading the gospel of rugby in schools and communities, looking like his soul was leaving his body, and every member of the press pack turned and glared at me, as if to say, 'You useful idiot.'

Those guys were big beasts of sports journalism – Stephen Jones of the *Sunday Times*, Chris Hewett of the *Independent*, Rob Kitson of the *Guardian*, Mick Cleary of the *Telegraph*, Tony Roche of the *Sun*, David Ferguson of the *Scotsman* – and I lost their respect there and then. I'm not sure I ever won it back.

Had things been going better for the Lions on the pitch, I might have had an easier ride, but I didn't have the experience or tools to interrogate events journalistically. And because those newspaper journalists had been around the block a thousand times, they could see how out of my depth I was, and they weren't the most forgiving bunch. There was certainly no one saying to me, 'Don't worry about making mistakes, just keep plugging away, you'll learn'; it was more a case of, 'What the hell is this kid doing here when he's clearly not up to snuff?'

And it wasn't just in the media briefings. One Lions activity involved a host of players being taken power boating and up in a helicopter to show them out and about and enjoying New Zealand. As part of this jamboree we were invited to interview some of the team on the experience and how they were finding the tour. Sitting down by the river, I was opposite one of the Test players, who was kindly giving me the textbook answers to textbook questions. That was all until one response, where he simply couldn't contain his laughter. His dissolving into hysterics had me utterly baffled, so I looked around to try and work out what I'd done, only to see a pair of his team-mate's bollocks resting on my shoulder. Lawyers, and his current high-profile position, prevent me from naming names.

The All Blacks ended up winning the series 3–0, making it a pretty miserable experience for British and Irish fans and media, but thankfully Graham was there for the Test matches, which started badly and got worse. The only high-light was the quite incredible performance of Dan Carter in the second Test in Wellington. I was mainly out and about reporting and gauging fan reaction, which as you can imagine just descended into a bit of a slog. And to be honest, by the time the final whistle on the last Test went, I think everyone was desperate to get out of there.

Because I'd been in New Zealand for so long, working non-stop, I had a lot of holiday to use up, so I decided to travel home from New Zealand via Brazil. As you do. I met a mate in Rio, went surfing up the coast, before heading to an amazing island four hours south and two hours off the coast called Ihla Grande. The island used to be a leper colony and was now a stunning nature reserve, with pristine rainforest and ivory-white beaches surrounded by a crystal-clear sea. I'm sure being a leper can't have been a picnic, but at least they had nice views.

The island's one hostel had two bunk beds left, and when we walked into the dorm, there on the floor was a complete Lions tour kit bag set with the initials 'SH'. We soon found out that SH stood for Ireland and Lions wing Shane Horgan, who had left the day before, giving all his stash to his mates who we then spent a week with. Having interviewed him half a dozen times over the previous 11 weeks, it was quite weird to travel to an island on the other side of the world and walk into his hostel. Seriously bizarre, especially as I had a very entertaining decade working alongside him at Sky, and he's now our Irish wheel at *The Good, The Bad & The Rugby*.

When I got home from South America, I joined Sky Sports News as a presenter. I'd spent countless hours on Brazilian beaches learning the *Rothmans Football Yearbook* back to front, when I could have been staring at bronzed Brazilians, and by the time I arrived for my first shift in my new role, I could tell you the home ground of every club in Britain, what their club crest looked like and who their record goal-scorer was, having known next to nothing beforehand.

I'm not sure reporting on the Lions tour knocked my confidence, or whether it made me realise just how much I had to learn, but stepping into the world of Sky Sports News was a whole extra level. I am a fair-weather football fan at best, so live rolling news on a football channel was a fast-moving travellator. Had social media existed back then, the public would have crucified me, because I made so many mistakes. And again, as a young kid who was probably further ahead than he should have been, I had to learn fast. It was a big old roster of presenters, some of whom had come from the major leagues and a few of whom were working their way up.

I will never forget how on one of my first shows I was working with a guy called Matt Lorenzo. He'd done break-fast telly, big sporting events and plenty of football and probably wondered why on earth he was working on a Wednesday morning shift with some ten-year-old who didn't know his Premier League. So when I went to the loo in an ad break, he turned the audio down on my talk back to the gallery. Not really knowing what on earth I was doing, when I ran back in, sat back down and plugged my earpiece in, I obviously didn't hear anything so picked my nose and drank my tea, waiting to be cued back from the break. I was oblivious to the fact we'd come back on air, and he left me hanging before asking if I fancied reading my lines. I'm not sure I made the same mistake again.

There was obviously a great gang as well, and with hindsight I learned a huge amount during the glory years of the channel. I was the apprentice to the likes of David Jones, Simon Thomas, Ed Chamberlin, Kirsty Gallagher, Kelly Cates and Georgie Thompson, all of whom I still see around and about, and all of whom have gone on to great things. But much of my early training was on the night shift with a telly god called David Bobin, who was more than three times my age and had been in journalism since the 1960s. We looked like a Werther's Original advert. David, who sadly passed away in 2017, always had a glass of red wine next to his desk and was completely unflappable. He was very much the skipper, in that if we hit turbulence, he'd take the controls and fly us through it. I'm not sure my broadcasting career would have gone any further had he not been my co-pilot. He was a great man, a rugby lover, and I learned a huge amount from him.

Because of my regular on-air blunders, my inexperience and the fact I looked ten, I was told from the start that I was miles away from being allowed to work on live sport, even rugby, and I should focus on learning how to broadcast. We'd do two hours between 10 p.m. and midnight, with the second hour recorded and played on a loop until 6 a.m., when morning presenters would pick up and take over again. As such, we wanted to make sure that second hour was as clean as possible. The mistakes eventually tailed off to a trickle, but I was only reading from the autocue.

One night, a couple of months into working it all out, one of the production crew came running into the gallery mid-shift and said, 'Alex, you're going to have to get yourself home. Simon Lazenby [the main rugby presenter at the time] is sick, we'll need you back in at 4.30 tomorrow morning to present the whole day's rugby.' So much for being miles away from being allowed to work on live sport …

To say I was slightly pumped up would be an understate-ment, so I only managed a couple of hours' sleep in the knowledge I'd be on air for 12 hours covering games from New Zealand, Australia, South Africa and Argentina with absolutely no preparation. I'll never forget sitting down in the studio next to All Blacks legend Sean Fitzpatrick, Wallabies legend Michael Lynagh, Springbok legend Bob Skinstad and England legend Will Greenwood, and feeling like I was standing on the highest diving board in the world. I distinctly remember wondering how on earth I had blagged my way into this position, alongside four legends, with no idea what I was meant to be talking about. The director's assistant keyed through to my ear piece, 'OK, Alex, we're on air in 20 seconds, 19, 18, 17, 16 …'

I took a big, deep breath, told myself this is what it had all been for and this was the moment. I told myself I was ready, and I could do it. At which point, Sean leant over, tapped me on the knee and said, 'Don't fuck it up, mate ...' 5, 4, 3, 2 ... I didn't have any choice but to jump.

It was undoubtedly my deep love of the game and knowledge of rugby that got me through that day. I hadn't prepared specifically for those games, but I followed the sport so closely that I knew the players and the storylines. And actually, by the end it felt like this was what I was meant to be doing. I learned that day that I could appear calm when I wasn't and could keep talking even when I couldn't find the exact words I wanted, which is useful for a live broadcaster. But it was like one of those days when a passenger manages to land a plane. It was just relief all round. Especially from me.

I thought I'd done OK in the circumstances, but it was difficult to tell. It's not as if people carried me out of the studio on their shoulders. But on the following Monday, a postcard arrived from Sky Sports managing director Vic Wakeling. Vic, a Fleet Street legend who had been with Sky Sports since its launch, was credited as the man who revolutionised sports broadcasting in the UK, so the words on that postcard meant a lot.

'Very good in trying circumstances, Vic,' was all it said, but it was like being patted on the shoulder by a broadcasting god. I still have that card. That's what you call man management.

11

A WORD FROM
OUR SPONSOR

HASK

If you'd told us a few years ago that *The Good, The Bad & The Rugby* would one day be sponsored by one of the top luxury drinks brands in the world, we'd have laughed like drains. At the start, our only realistic hook-up would've been with Blue Nun and even then we'd have had to buy our own bottles. Fast forward to now, and somehow we're in cahoots with Rémy Martin, purveyors of premier cognac since 1724. I mean, I'd take a free keyring from Greggs, so this was a bit of a coup.

Now, let's be honest: cognac in Britain has always had an image problem. It's not something you knock back on a Friday at Infernos, is it? It's your nan's Christmas tipple, usually lit on fire before anyone actually drinks it. Before Rémy came calling, I'd already trained my palate on the 'supposedly finest' things in life such as cigars, whisky, and overpriced cheese that smells like your socks after a gym session, so I'd learned to appreciate cognac. But most people here? They'd rather stick to Jägerbombs.

The brand wanted to change that 'exclusive and mysterious' vibe, and to stop being the drink of choice for French aristocrats and rappers with diamond-encrusted chalices. And who better to achieve that than us three idiots? Honestly, if you want to make something look accessible, plonk it next to Alex, Tins and me.

To kick things off, they flew us out to the estate in Cognac. Poor Tins had no idea it was made from grapes, he thought it came from reconstituted Christmas puddings or something. So we began in the vineyards. Then it was off to the distillery: a cavernous lair of metal tanks full of fermenting wine. I half-expected Roger Moore in a safari suit to pop out, pursued by henchmen in hazmat suits wielding laser beams.

Max, our guide, explained that nine litres of wine become one litre of *eaux de vie*, 'the water of life'. Romantic, isn't it? From there, it's aged in oak casks for years, sometimes decades. The cellars were stacked with thousands, like an IKEA for alcoholics. At the top end you've got Louis XIII, a blend of up to 1,200 *eaux de vie*, aged 40–100 years. A bottle sets you back £3k. I once had a single glass that cost £250 to celebrate the end of a season and a good year for me. It was amazing, but I didn't drink it the right way and it was not served correctly either, so might as well have been Ribena. However, now I get how to drink it, it's a totally different experience.

Of course, when you're charging car-money for booze, your *maître de chai* has to make sure every bottle tastes identical. Wine can vary from year to year. Cognac? No excuses. If someone drops £3k and it tastes like petrol, you're toast.

Now, tasting cognac is like wine tasting: lots of theatre, lots of waffling, everyone desperately trying to sound like the late Sir Michael Winner. Max would say 'apricots', and Alex would immediately parrot, 'Yes, mmm apricots!' He said 'nutmeg', Alex said, 'Yes, I was thinking nutmeg.' He is such a teacher's pet. However, Max having assured us that there were no wrong suggestions, Alex made the terrible mistake of trying to think for himself. He got all giddy and tried to show off, And having suggested that he was getting hints of vanilla, Max promptly told him that that couldn't be the case.

I piped up with, 'So you can get it wrong,' which Max conceded Alex had.

Cue me then chiming in with the fact I was getting hints of apple, which Max agreed and said, 'Yes, apple, *très bien* James, you really have a refined palate.' Ha! Point to Haskell. I gave Alex the middle finger while no one was looking. You always have to celebrate your wins against Alex.

Max particularly wanted to demonstrate Rémy's versatility and fun, to which end he had us making cocktails. First up was a Rémy Ginger, which was Rémy VSOP, ginger ale, a couple of dashes of Angostura Bitters and some lemon zest. And of course, because everything with *GBR* has to be turned into a bloody competition, Max decided we'd all have a go at making our own Rémy Ginger. Now, I was particularly keen to shine, as I was genuinely a fan of Rémy. So I followed the instructions meticulously. Measured, stirred, lemon zest at the right angle: it was basically cocktail-making foreplay.

But here's the thing: Max went all giddy schoolgirl around Tins. He tasted mine, pulled a face like I'd just served him a pint of diesel, and said it was awful despite the fact I'd done exactly what he'd bloody told me to. Then, surprise, surprise, he crowns Tins the winner. Oh of course! Because what better way to curry favour with the royal family than handing the big man a rosette for best cocktail? I half expected him to bow and ask for a knighthood on the spot.

I didn't let it slide. I told Max straight: 'You're not getting the Légion d'honneur out of this, mate. And if you stitch me up again, you'll be lucky to make it out of this vineyard alive.'

But in fairness, it was a cracking day. Booze flowing, banter flying, and me, once again, robbed of victory by the gravitational pull of Tindall's royal connections.

The drinking was not done there. Max served us Rémy Old Fashioneds, made with VSOP rather than the traditional bourbon. You'd want to make sure that someone else was paying, but I can report that it is quite delightful, my new personal favourite.

I know a lot of bollocks is spoken about alcohol, but that tasting session completely changed the way I thought about cognac. Beforehand, I could understand why cognac slightly worried people, because it has a reputation as an overpowering spirit that makes you shudder. But having tried it in four or five different ways, and not shuddered once, I can report that drunk at the right time, in the right way, cognac is as accessible as any other spirit, only more luxurious. I've become a bit of a cognac evangelical and have even got my mum into it. Having not liked the stuff at all, she's now a big fan.

And yes, I was suspiciously well-behaved with the sponsor. Alex and Tins said they'd never seen me be so complimentary, but when you're giving me free bottles, darling, I'm basically yours.

We were staying in a nice hotel with a couple of the Rémy guys, while the rest of our crew were in town. But while our crew usually make do with a Tesco meal deal on a shoot day, and a bag of Haribo Tangfastics if they're feeling extravagant, this time they got to join us for a bona fide feast laid on by Rémy: more oysters than you could shake a stick at, the finest regional cheeses and meats, pig trotters, foie gras, and, as you would expect, a shit load of cognac.

Young people who work in TV tend to be quite progressive in their sensibilities, and I could see that a few of them were quite alarmed by all this decadence, especially the foie gras. To those guys, eating the fatty liver of a force-fed goose is one of the quickest ways to hell, whereas I can't eat anything that hasn't suffered. Sometimes, I want to know in detail how it's suffered. And I didn't want people making me feel sad while I was tucking into my foie gras, so I asked if they could all turn around and face the wall.

I jest, of course. In truth, all morals went out of the window and they fell upon the feast like ravenous peasants (not surprising, really, seeing as they hadn't eaten for about 18 hours), and once they'd finished making themselves sick into a bucket, like Mr Creosote from Monty Python's *The Meaning of Life*, I said to them, 'This meal has ruined you lot forever.' 'What do you mean?' 'You've been ruined, darlings. Absolutely ruined. Because up until now, you genuinely thought the pinnacle of culinary decadence was

Harvester. The salad bar! The bacon bits! The Thousand Island dressing slopped on like Dulux! Maybe, if you were really pushing the boat out, a mixed grill with a pint of lukewarm Fosters. And that was your Everest. That was you saying, "This is as good as life gets."

'Well, it isn't.

'I remember the first time I was taken to Nobu. Oh my word. The entire axis of my world shifted. One bite of black cod in miso, and I knew: my life of Beefeater pubs and cheeky Nando's meal deals was over. Spoiled. Corrupted. Ruined forever.

'And now it's happened to you. You'll never again be able to look at a Harvester salad bar with misty-eyed joy. If it's not foie gras and caviar, darling, you're going to be scowling. When the waiter plonks down your chips and gravy, you'll be sitting there muttering, "Where's the lobster thermidor, please?"

'I'm afraid it's irreversible. You've had a taste of the high life, and you'll never be happy with a Nando's medium spice again.'

We all got extremely drunk that night, and I'd made the mistake of riding a hired bike to the restaurant from my hotel. In daylight, following a local who knew where he was going, that was OK. At night, after a skinful, giving a grown man a backie, with no street lights, was a very different proposition. One hand on the bars, the other on my phone doubling as both map and torch, I nearly rode into walls, cars, ditches. Not even joking I did seriously almost die, as I could not see where I was going and almost went off the road down a huge drop into a river. It was a very sobering moment; I was on my own, thinking *Fucking hell, James, that could have been it.* At one point I stumbled across a gang of lads smoking weed and thought I was about to be mugged. The fact I had a child seat on the back of the bike didn't help – it made me look like the Child Catcher in *Chitty Chitty Bang Bang* on his day off. Thank God I'd left the big net and boiled sweets at the hotel.

We all made it home alive. The crew, previously cognac virgins, were now swigging it like Ribena. It felt like we'd broken the spell of exclusivity. Well it certainly had for me, although in truth, for the rest of the team I think it was just because it was free. If they had been handing out meths, our lot would have got into it.

12

○

QUITE A FUNNY BUNCH

PAYNO

In 2025, TV is no longer the undisputed king and its voice is no longer as dominant as it once was. Instead, anybody can tell a story to anyone who wants to listen, content comes at you from everywhere, and a lot of sports organisations are more interested in having online influencers presenting at their events than experienced broadcasters and former athletes who have been there and done it, because they think they're more likely to connect with youngsters. With a 15- and a 12-year-old, I have no problem with that.

Sports organisations and broadcasters would say they're just reacting to a changing environment, that people want immediacy and brevity rather than more in-depth stuff that might take days to put together and requires some thought. But I do think there will always be an audience who want it done 'properly', with authoritative opinions from people who've been in the cauldron. Sometimes the current audience is being ignored as broadcasters chase new audiences.

One of my mentors at Sky was Graham Simmons, who I'm sure nostalgic readers of this book will remember as a brilliant storyteller on our rugby coverage. As I mentioned earlier, Simmo was one of the best in the business at what he did, crafting the most amazing interviews and features. Much like ITV's Gabriel Clarke, Simmo asked questions that took people to places they hadn't expected to go and elicited answers that revealed a person's character; he had a great way with words, and his features were beautifully put together, with clever lines that made you think married to the perfect images. They certainly weren't things you could create on a phone and then slap on TikTok.

While Martin Turner was the man who said, 'Right, here's the mic, let's see what you can do,' Simmo was the man who taught me how to do it better. He wasn't the kind of person who put an arm around juniors and said, 'This is how you do it, son,' but you'd learn a huge amount from him by just watching and listening.

Simmo was in his pomp when touchlines teemed with journalists, people who weren't afraid to ask difficult questions at difficult moments. In those days there was a bit of needle between reporters, coaches and players, and it made for great telly. But the game has changed – players are media trained, clubs can ban access and truthfully – I'm not sure audiences want touchline interrogation any more. So there are more 'Sum up your feelings' and 'Can you take any positives?' rather than 'Was that acceptable?' and 'Do changes need to be made?'

That old-school craft hasn't disappeared, because there are still some unbelievable sports documentaries being made and some of the camerawork on live sport is an art in itself. But just when I was beginning to think that rugby had lost all its big characters, they started making their own content, and some of it is rather good.

Before the Premiership final in 2025, Bath back-row Miles Reid created a really cool piece of content that he posted on his Instagram account. I stopped what I was doing and watched the whole thing, and the thought occurred to me that maybe more players will start learning the skills to tell their own stories and put their own perspectives across, which is very exciting.

Younger players do get affected by criticism, but they aren't as afraid of online trolls as older players, so they're more inclined to share. And I think player content channels will really help drive awareness of and interest in the game (although it might put a few of the clubs' media managers out of jobs).

Sportspeople finding their own voices has certainly made it a tougher environment for sports journalists in general, because it means stars and fans can bypass them completely. Journalists used to be regarded as pillars of authority and write whatever they wanted, and there was no comeback from the athletes, because they didn't have the channels. But now they're almost all on social media, and when there are two competing narratives – a sportsperson's and a journalist's – fans will usually take the side of the sportsperson, because they're the ones performing heroics every week.

I will never forget the clearest indication of just how quickly the power shifted. I was on Sky Sports News one evening, and part of the final hour was always a look ahead to the following day's back pages. There was a huge splash on one of the red tops shouting 'Wayne Rooney set to leave Man Utd', which we covered. Almost immediately, Rooney put out a tweet saying 'I'm not going anywhere, I've just signed a new deal with Man Utd.' The paper hadn't even hit the newsstands, but already the story was dead, killed by the player himself.

When it comes to the criticism, I'm often reminded of that famous speech by former American president Teddy Roosevelt, which begins: 'It is not the critic who counts; not the man who points out how the strong man stumbles, or where the doer of deeds could have done them better. The credit belongs to the man who is actually in the arena, whose face is marred by dust and sweat and blood.'

I think another reason we're seeing more characters emerging in rugby – like Henry Pollock, his England and Lions team-mates Tommy Freeman and Fin Smith – is because they don't read newspapers like previous generations did. They don't care what Stephen Jones or Stuart Barnes said about them in *The Times*, or what player rating the *Telegraph* gave them, but they might listen to *The Good, The Bad & The Rugby*, or watch *Squidge Rugby* on YouTube.

They're more likely to engage with newer media because they're less likely to feel judged. Newspaper interviewers can't help putting their own spin on things, while podcasts give sportspeople the space to just tell their story. And for every newspaper article arguing that Henry Pollock, for example, should be dropped, there will now be four or five YouTube montages of Henry Pollock's greatest moments gaining many more clicks.

Having been at Sky when the rugby rights drained away, I have some sympathy for the print journalists out there. They must be wrestling with a challenging environment, and even during the Lions tour this year two or three of them were told their job was up. Occasionally, they'll pop up on WhatsApp, after the latest episode of *The Good, The Bad & The Rugby* has just been aired, and our interview with RFU chief executive Bill Sweeney got a few of them frothing at the mouth.

Bill was copping it from all angles, the consensus in the press being that his recent pay packet, which included a large bonus, was a disgrace given that the RFU was losing money, RFU employees were being laid off and the England men's team still wasn't close to being the best in the world. He was, understandably, getting a lot of heat. So I asked if he wanted to come on the pod – not for an easy ride, but to respond to some of what was being thrown at him in his own words. We have always said we're not *Newsnight*, but we covered as many topics as we could in 90 minutes, and did so in a conversation rather than an interrogation. Many said they saw a different side of the story, some said we're RFU puppets. I just wanted a decent debate with a decent man. It's not life or death, after all.

A few days later, a well-known sports journalist wrote a column that was fairly critical of our interview. He essentially accused us of giving Bill an easy ride and asking the 'wrong' questions. Now of course everyone's entitled to their opinion. But my thought was, 'If you've got all the right questions, and you've got 30 years of sporting journalistic credibility, what does it say when you can't get an interview with the RFU CEO?' Has the landscape changed, are people wanting more control over their own words, and what is the role of the written media nowadays?

Newspaper journalists are always kicking off about the lack of access they get, and the Lions tour of 2025 was another example where relations between the press pack and the Lions media team was tepid at best. I think my perspective comes from the fact I've never really been agenda-driven. It's not been in my role, but I've also never quite understood the 'Sack him now' angle. When Eddie Jones was fired by England, a fairly prominent journalist was overheard saying, 'We got the fucker out', which made me think, *What game are you playing? Whatever it is, I don't understand the rules.*

As I said, I've always found Bill Sweeney to be a really decent man, and I don't think he's the reason the game in England has all the challenges it has. It doesn't really matter who you appoint to run English rugby because the problem is the set-up. It's run by a thousand parish councils, and while there are some great people among them, too many are worrying about the rhododendrons, what hymns should be played in church and where their trestle table will be located at the village fete. And Bill is at the top of all that, God help him.

Bill is obviously a skilful sports politician, but he's also riding about ten horses at once. He's responsible for everything from grass-roots tag rugby to line-managing the England head coach. He also represents the RFU in relation to World Rugby, European Professional Club Rugby, the Six Nations and the Lions.

That's why I thought the media fuss over Bill's pay packet was slightly unfair. Bill got the bonuses he did because he hit certain targets he was asked to hit, and that's just what administrators at the sharp end of sport get paid. If they got rid of Bill, they'd have to replace him with someone on a similar wage. It's not a charity, and it's a gigantic job, so the best wouldn't do it for less.

Bill did concede that the RFU wasn't the best at getting its message out there – it made a mess of communicating the lowering of the tackle height in 2023 – and I think that led to an erosion of trust. And because its relationship with many mainstream media outlets broke down, which meant it couldn't get its messaging out that way, and it wasn't brave enough to say what it really thought on its own channels, a vacuum opened up, which was filled by people wanting to put their own spin on things. Which was where our pod came in. *The Good, The Bad & The Rugby* is a platform for people to tell their side of the story. Obviously, we could have given Bill a really rough ride, Paxman style, but he'd never have wanted to engage with us again. The reality is that a lot of the drama was fabricated, idealistic and based on black and white. But that's not reality. And at the risk of repeating myself, perhaps it's worth exploring why newspaper journalists are unable to nail him down for a chat.

TINS

On my early tours with England, journalists would stay in the same hotel as us, and we'd have a chat with them in the bar. But Clive Woodward, who grew wary of the media, changed all that towards the end of his time in charge.

At the 2003 World Cup we were sweeping our changing rooms for bugs, and we trained behind a black wall so no one could see. Clive was always saying, 'Don't give our opponents a headline, something that writes their team talk for them,' and players would run through possible questions the night before a game and come up with the 'right' answers.

I was quite personable, always polite to journalists, but I did as I was told, which forced me along a road I wouldn't have gone down otherwise. I could have had a far better relationship with the media, but having been told to be wary, I didn't want to give them anything.

Now, I look back and think, *That wasn't the best way of doing things*, because it didn't allow us to reveal our personalities, and rugby was crying out for big personalities. Rugby has always been about the team and therefore had issues with players being themselves, but that's the wrong way of looking at it. Players being themselves create hype and make the game more valuable.

Guys like Joe Marler and Hask polarise people – some love them, some don't – but there's nothing wrong with that. American player Ilona Maher has gone from 250k Instagram followers to 5 million in the last couple of years, and it had little to do with winning a bronze medal at the 2024 Olympics. She's unashamedly herself on social media, is a big advocate of body positivity, has appeared on *Dancing with the Stars* and in the swimsuit edition of *Sports Illustrated*, and gave a great speech about women's rugby and sport in general at the 2025 ESPY Awards. That's how things should be done.

There has been a shift in rugby in the last couple of years, but it's come too late for a lot of players, Jonny May being the best example. Jonny is one of the quirkiest guys I've ever met, but hardly anyone would have known that until he retired, started appearing on *The Good, The Bad & The Rugby* and talked about his experiences. Jonny would say that he didn't want anyone focusing on his personality while he was still playing, but him opening up about his neurodivergence has really struck a chord with people, and he could have been doing that all the way through his career.

Of course, the modern sportsperson can directly connect with fans through social media and only interact with traditional media when they really need to. The upside of that shift is that they no longer have to deal with journalists who like to put their spin on interviews; the downside is that social media is full of people who like to rant and rave about anything and everything. But younger players who have only ever known social media are better at switching off the negativity than us older players were. Saying that, scanning replies to a social media post can be useful, because occasionally someone makes a fair point and I think about making adjustments.

13

THE GREATEST FEMALE DARTS PLAYER OF ALL TIME?

HASK

Bodhi will come into my bedroom most mornings, take her nappy off and put it in the bin (she's potty trained during the day, not so much after that). I'll tell her to shut the door before she climbs into bed with me, and depending on what mood she's in, she'll face the wall and go to sleep or cuddle up to me.

If it's the latter, I'll say, 'Can we go back to sleep?' And on a good day, we'll sleep until maybe 7.30. But on a not so good day, it's anywhere between 5.30 or 6.30 when she has walked in. She'll keep saying, 'Daaaaady, I want nilk (meaning milk).'

'I can't give you milk,' I'll reply, 'but I can give you food in a bit.'

'But Daaaaady, I want nilk.'

'Bodhi, no. Can we go back to sleep please?'

'Daaaaady, can we go downstairs?'

'Bodhi, please just go to sleep ...'

'OK, Daddy ...'

Thirty seconds later, she'll be trying to open my eyes. Then she'll say, 'Daaaaady, I love you. You're my best friend.'

'Come on then, let's get up,' I'll say, and she'll drag me to the kitchen.

Now Bodhi's a gorgeous child, divine in every way, except, of course, she eats like she's on hunger strike. I swear, she could sit at a Michelin-starred tasting menu and turn her nose up until you offered her a buttered bagel. Honestly, I don't know where she gets it from. Neither Chloe nor I are fussy. I'll eat anything. Put olives, offal, or an actual armadillo in front of me and I'll have a crack. My motto has always been 'try it before you slag it off'.

But Bodhi? She declares she dislikes things before they've even entered the room. Chocolate? Didn't want it. Sweets? Absolutely not. Biscuits? Flat refusal. I had to physically demonstrate, like some deranged dessert sommelier: 'Look, darling, Daddy's eating the biscuit and not dying.' Only then would she nibble a millimetre of it and realise it was fine.

So, over the years I've explained to her: 'Daddy will never give you anything horrid. I'm not slipping you anchovies in the night, I'm just trying to give you the good stuff.' Eventually I got her onto burgers (a triumph), lamb burgers (even better), and vegetable rice (my Michelin-star moment). But my word, it's a battle. Eating out? Stressful. She is definitely getting better, and the difference from when I started this book to where she is now is night and day.

At home we've got a routine. Breakfast is a yoghurt (she initially resisted, now she loves them), or a buttered bagel. Coco Pops are tolerated but dry only. Milk is apparently the devil unless consumed from a bottle. Taking her out is

trickier, but she adores the chicken sausages at Ginger &
White in Hampstead. So off we go, me trying to look serene
and middle-class with a flat white, her sat opposite like a
live hand grenade with the pin out.

To keep the child from detonating I put something on my
phone for her to watch. I try *Bluey*. I love *Bluey*. It's genius.
But no, Bodhi wants *Cocomelon*, which is nothing short of
industrial-strength mind-rot. It's like being waterboarded
with nursery rhymes. Then she moves on to *Blippi*, which is
marginally less awful, but still not ideal viewing for a
40-year-old man trying to eat chorizo scrambled egg and
bagel. I once tried to slip in *Family Guy* instead. It actually
went down really well, and I loved it, but I realised after that
it was not age appropriate. In any way. Who knew? Well,
the parents that would tut at me when they saw me watching it with her – I mean, they knew.

Books, though, are my salvation. I've stolen a trick from
the internet: 'You want a treat? You read a book.' Obviously
she can't read yet but when she can that is my plan, but I
read to her every single night. Non-negotiable. And not the
same bloody book on repeat either, or I'll lose the will to
live. So we're regulars at Waterstones. *The Gruffalo*, *The
Tiger Who Came to Tea* are classics. *Spot the Dog* pop-ups
are great too.

I've told Bodhi I have a pet dragon called Archie who
lives in the loft and eats foxes and naughty cats, which she
thinks is amazing. Archie is black and gold. She insists she
has her own dragon called Arna, and she is black and purple.
I've told her mine's better. Obviously, Bodhi is having none
of it and tells me with one fist curled that she will fight me.

After which I have to back down and concede that perhaps Arna is better.

I'm a big believer in doing things with kids. Not just parking them in front of *Cocomelon* until their eyes glaze over. Bodhi's at nursery most of the time, but when she's with me I don't like just sitting around the house. No, we're out. We're exploring. We're adventuring. She loves animals and dinosaurs, so it's the Natural History Museum, petting zoos, city farms anywhere that's vaguely Jurassic or smells faintly of manure.

Of course, if it's raining, then it's soft play. Now, soft play is a particular hazard for me. I like to get involved, you see, but I'm not exactly built for plastic tunnels and foam rollers. Former rugby player, built like a fridge-freezer, it's not a natural fit. Every time I crawl in, I have visions of being stuck and having to feature on one of those old TV reconstructions, like *999*: 'Here we see James Haskell, former England flanker, being cut free from a giant plastic slide as children look on in horror.' Not quite the legacy I had in mind.

Farms are safer, in theory at least. Bodhi adores feeding the animals. I feed the big horses, she feeds the little ones, and then it's pigs, cows, the lot. But her absolute favourite? Chickens. Or as she calls them, 'cockadoos'. She is obsessed. When they crow, she lights up like it's the greatest show on Earth.

But of course, one day disaster struck. I didn't see her little hand sneak through a cage and one cockadoo gave her finger a good nip. Cue meltdown. Now she eyes them with the suspicion of a Victorian street urchin.

Horses, too, have been a trial. I showed her how to feed them 'flat hand, darling, flat hand' but she's only three, so it's in one ear, out the other. Sure enough, the horse snaffled and nipped her fingers. You've never seen such apoplexy. I had to go into full hostage-negotiator mode just to calm her down.

And then, because fate clearly enjoys humiliating me, a sheep nicked an entire bag of feed pellets right out of her hands. She stood there outraged, betrayed, and I thought: *Yes darling, welcome to life. Animals, like people, will take whatever you've got if you're not careful.*

So yes, the girl's learning. Sometimes the hard way. But that's what it's all about, isn't it? Farms, fun, cockadoos and the occasional horse bite.

She doesn't nap anymore, which is tragic for me at the weekend, not her. I'd kill for a nap. The weekday schedule goes like this: make her lunch, bundle her off to nursery, graft until 6 p.m., pick her up, cook tea, shower, bedtime routine. She bloody loves nursery and cannot get enough of it. She comes back every day slightly more grown up, which is terrifying.

The bedtime routine is treated like it's a seamless military operation. In reality, it's me cramming into her tiny bed, half hanging off like I'm auditioning for *I'm a Celebrity: Get Me Out of This Cabin Bed*. I'll say, 'Bodhi, can you budge up?' and she'll shift her knees two inches while keeping her head planted slap-bang in the middle. 'Sorry, Daddy – too big.' And that's it. I'm condemned to cling on like a rock climber without ropes while trying to read *Spot the Dog*. She has got better, to the point now where she says, 'Look, Daddy,

I budge up,' and yes there is more space in her adult single. It's still not ideal, but there has been progress and, either way, I love it. These times at night when we go up together, she gets undressed – well she tries and then has a meltdown when she can't do it, but I say, 'You can,' and after tears and moaning, she finally does it – and we celebrate and cuddle. Always celebrate the little wins.

We then brush our teeth together, I take her into her room, try not to break her bed and then read her a story. I kiss her goodnight and shut the door. Then you would think it's rest time for me, but sadly not, it's only then that my work day starts.

I've got Bodhi just shy of half the time. When it's the two of us, it's bliss. But as soon as she sees her mum, then it's Daddy who? Which is fine, because Chloe and I are a great team and can do meals together with her and other activities. When you separate from a partner and you have a kid, it's not about you anymore, it's about your children; you have to overcome your egos and put them first. It's a challenge, it's hard, things go wrong, but if you can do it then the winners are the children 100 per cent.

We try to be a team, and Bodhi loves it when we are together. It takes work and compromise but it's the only way I want to do it. Bodhi is the most important thing to both of us.

When my dad died, Chloe picked her up for me when I was supposed to, as I couldn't get back in time for nursery pick-up, and we all went out as a family. That meant the world. Because whatever happens between adults, the child comes first. Always.

And my God, the older Bodhi gets, the sharper she gets. She's three going on 13. Social as anything, fiercely possessive about her friends. She'll meet a new one and immediately turn to me with: 'No, Daddy, go away!' Charming. She looks and acts a year older, and she's got this weirdly wise little brain. Which, frankly, puts me under pressure. I feel like I have to make every second of every day with her perfect, enriching, magical, Instagrammable, when sometimes all she really wants is a chicken sausage and an episode of *Cocomelon*.

I still feel like we're never doing enough and it's that parent guilt about juggling work, your life and being a good parent. I'll hear other parents talking about their kids getting various belts in judo or karate, or learning to play a Chopin nocturne on the piano, and I'll think, *Shit, what if Bodhi's a child prodigy and I didn't allow her to discover her greatest talent? Maybe she could have been the greatest female darts player of all time?*

Of course, it's not realistic to think like that. You want to give your children your undivided attention, and I try to condense most of my work into the three days a week I don't have her, but it's not always easy trying to be full steam ahead with work and not picking up your phone. Plus, kids don't always do what you want them to do anyway. Sometimes Bodhi is in a mischievous mood, sometimes she's ill, sometimes she just can't be bothered. But she's a very well-adjusted kid and I have the best time with her, which is all you can really hope for.

I wish my body wasn't creaking as much as it is, because even running after Bodhi or playing football with her is hard. Actually, I struggle just to walk properly. I used to have good and bad days, but now it's just bad days. I'm due to have an operation where they'll fuse the small subtalar joint in my ankle which will mean I am off my feet for two weeks and then ten weeks of rehab. I can't pick Bodhi up sometimes because my wrist aches due to an old scaphoid injury, and I can't do a press-up unless it's on my knuckles, very Rocky-esque but not that useful at times. I actually had the screw out the other day as it was put in when I was 21 after winning the Middlesex Sevens, but sadly over time it had started to cause pain, arthritis and upset the workings of the other bones.

But I don't regret anything or hold any grudges. The only person I blame for all my ailments is myself, because I agreed to play with anaesthetic and cortisone injections – and rugby has given me an amazing life.

14

JEKYLL AND HYDES

TINS

Nigel Melville was Gloucester's head coach when I signed for them, but by the time I joined, he'd been replaced by Dean Ryan – and I didn't think he was a fan of mine.

Actually, I knew he wasn't a fan of mine, because his old Bristol team-mate Garath Archer had told me so (Dean and Arch were a semi-psychotic lock pairing who had it in for my old mate Tom May for reasons unbeknown to me. One of their line-out moves was even called Tom May and involved Dean and Arch coming round the corner and running straight at whoever the centre was that day. If it was actually Tom May, all the better).

Dean's distaste for me stemmed from a game between Bath and Bristol at the Rec a few years earlier. I had passed the ball to Balsh, who had done what he normally did and skinned their 13 on the outside, and I went hurtling down the middle of the field, to make it a one-on-one against their full-back. Reacting to the situation, Dean pulled me back by the collar, back when there weren't enough cameras to spot that kind of thing, only for Balsh to skin the full-back and score on his own. I turned around and gave Dean a load of verbals, at which point his eyes changed. He looked like he wanted to kill me.

Dean had boxed in the Army, and he spent the next 40 minutes chasing me around the field trying to fill me in. When I tried to steal a ball, he came flying in and hit me with an uppercut, right on the tip of the chin. I said to him, 'I thought you were a boxer? You can't have won many fights if that's how hard you hit,' and steam started coming out of his ears.

A few minutes later, he cleaned me out at a ruck and smashed his forearm into my face. That one hurt a little bit more, but this time I said to him, 'Yep, you definitely don't hit hard. Did you used to hit them with your handbag?' A few minutes after that, he got yellow-carded, and I waved him off with a smile and a little song.

After the game, Garath Archer said to me, 'What did you do to Dean? He fucking hates you!', and those words were ringing in my ears the first day I turned up for training with Gloucester. I was genuinely worried, so I went to Dean and told him what Arch had told me, which was the best thing I could have done. Dean explained that while his emotions could go from 0 to 60 in no time, the next day he'd have forgotten all about whatever had set him off. That initial disagreement and follow-up chat actually ended up being good for our relationship, because I could always tell how pissed off he really was.

It's amazing how much someone can change when they walk onto a rugby field, and I played with quite a few Jekyll and Hydes during my career. The most extreme case was probably South African centre Robbie Fleck, who I first encountered playing for England against the Springboks at Twickenham in 2002. We absolutely killed them that day, running out 53–3 winners, but my abiding memory is how incredibly dirty South Africa were.

You can watch the highlights on YouTube, and it's like rugby from the 1970s, with cheap shots all over the field. Jannes Labuschagne is sent off for a late tackle on Jonny Wilkinson, Norman Jordaan tries to strangle me at the bottom of a ruck, Werner Greef almost takes Phil Christophers' head off, while skipper Corne Krige loses the plot completely. He stamps on Phil Vickery, knees Lawrence Dallaglio, elbows Jason Robinson, punches Wilko twice, headbutts Matt Dawson and elbows Martin Johnson in the face, which was never a wise thing to do. To top it all off, Krige also tries to take Daws' head off but connects with his own fly-half André Pretorius instead, ending his game.

At one point, Robbie pinned me to the floor and screamed, 'I hate you! I wanna kill your family! I hate you!' And I thought, *I'm not sure that's acceptable* … I didn't shake his hand after the game, and as far as I was concerned, he was an absolute nutter who had said something he could never make up for. But a few months later, my Bath coaches John 'Knuckles' Connolly and Anthony Foley told me they were thinking of signing him. I said to them, 'If he joins, I'm leaving, the bloke's an absolute tool and I don't want to play with him.' A few months after that, the club announced that Robbie would be joining us the following season.

Knuckles and Anthony kept trying to reassure me, telling me how well they thought Robbie and I would work together in the centres, but I still thought it was bullshit. Then Robbie turned up for his first training session and he was the nicest man you could possibly meet. I couldn't get my head around it and felt the need to ask him what he remembered about 'that' game. He looked slightly embarrassed, said he'd lost control because they were playing terrible and getting pumped and team-mates had given up and he couldn't handle it, but then assured me he was a changed man. Readers, he was not a changed man …

Robbie was a great player, and we did work well together in the centres, but if someone wronged him – said something, hit him late, trod on him – he'd go rogue and spend the next five minutes chasing the guy around the field. I'd remind him that his job wasn't to carry out personal vendettas, it was to get back in the line and be in the right position for the next phase of play, and he'd explain that the red mist had descended and apologise. But ten minutes later, he'd be chasing someone else who'd wronged him. In the end, I'd clap in his face and say, 'Robbie, back in the room! Stop chasing him around the field! You can sort that personal thing out when the game's over.'

Having thought I despised him, Robbie and I ended up being great friends. On the field, he might threaten to kill your family; off it, he was one of the most relaxed blokes you could meet and a really nice human being.

15

BRAIN FART

PAYNO

Having been forced to post me on the front line, the bosses soon realised that I was slightly better at presenting live rugby than I was at presenting sports news, and by the end of the first 12 months I'd begun to settle into the chair. Then I got another surprising break.

In 2008, the number two rugby presenter after Simon Lazenby was a fantastically charismatic Welsh guy called Rhodri Williams. Rhodri was a brilliant man – a huge presence with a roaring laugh and a deep love of Wales. As well as being a TV presenter, he owned a nightclub in Cardiff called the Cameo Club, and I spent many hours alongside him on Sky Sports News in the early days. He was forever online buying paper towels and multi-packs of Bacardi Breezers in between the interviews and reading the autocue. And I will never forget the time he came in for an early evening shift, straight from Wales beating England at Twickenham. He had, to put it mildly, had a rather good day, arrived minutes before we went on air, cut himself shaving in the hurry to get ready and so presented with wet tissue on his chin. Not a word out of place over the three hours, and I think he'd just about sobered up when we came off air. I was in awe.

Unfortunately for Rhodri, he ended up having a very large night out with Scottish celebrity John Leslie, at a time when the 'shamed ex-Blue Peter presenter', as he was known in the media, was tabloid fodder. Rhodri got caught in the crossfire, ended up on the front pages – where wholesome Sky Sports presenters are not meant to be – and he left via the backdoor. As a man who's lived a thousand lives, he headed off for his next adventure but his departure left the rugby department a man down.

I'm sure there were some fairly raised eyebrows at my rapid transformation from tea boy to presenter, but there was also a lot of support. Everyone in sport knows, if they give you the shirt, you play, and don't spend any time worrying about the guys who missed out. Looking back, I was a bit like an unflushable turd, in that I just kept bobbing about, so that people couldn't ignore me. I hope I wasn't irritatingly relentless, but I was definitely a trier. It should say on my gravestone: HERE LIES ALEX PAYNE – HE PERSEVERED.

As for the media reaction, the only comment from those early days that springs to mind was by veteran *Daily Mail* journalist Alan Fraser, who wrote that I made him feel 'impossibly old'. To be fair, he also said that I could do the job 'competently', and I've certainly had a lot worse written about me since.

More intimidating than journalists who thought I looked too young were angry coaches who thought I looked too young. Some of the hardest things I've done in broadcasting are post-match interviews with coaches whose sides have just lost, including Steve Diamond, who gave me a real going over when he was a coach at Saracens. I forget the details, but his tone was, 'You look about 15, you don't deserve to be here, you obviously don't know what you're talking about,' and everything I asked came straight back off the middle of his bat.

A few years later I hosted a dinner for him, and he couldn't have been more supportive. We preach weekly that the game needs big characters and big talking points but I can tell you being among them is not easy, particularly when they're fuming. At least nowadays I'd have the experience and confidence to justify the questions I was asking, but when you're learning your craft, still in awe of the environment, and not quite sure which end of the microphone to hold, you're likely to crumble as soon as they push back at you.

In 2012, Simon Lazenby left to present Formula 1, and after a bit of a talent parade, I was given the role of Sky Sports Rugby's lead presenter. I'd been champing at the bit to take over from Simon for a while, so I was initially ecstatic. But then I started thinking, *Christ, I've got the gig. Am I good enough to do this? Have I got what it takes?*

Simon had come up through the ranks in the same way I had – runner, production assistant, Sky Sports News presenter to lead rugby presenter. He was a master of his craft, always in control but still relishing the moments when it all went wrong. He was pretty laid-back in the way he went about the role, and because he didn't do hours of prep like me, I always thought he wasn't that interested. But it wasn't complacency; he was just very comfortable doing what he was doing. He had the battle scars, for sure, but he'd got to the stage where he was great at the job with very little effort, with his hard work going into interests outside of work. In other words, presenting wasn't his be-all and end-all.

My first up-close exposure to 'presenters' was Tim Lovejoy on *Soccer AM*, and he was unquestionably the star of the show. He drove it and everything revolved around him. But that was never going to be the job spec I wanted, first because that's not my personality, second because I was always told to be a facilitator, someone who gets the best out of guests and makes them look as good as possible. Mostly I just teed them up and watched them hit, and rugby pundits tended to go in harder back then. Somebody like Stuart Barnes had very strong opinions, and wasn't afraid of offending anyone, which made for good television.

The jump from number two to number one presenter was far bigger than I was expecting, and I certainly felt the increased pressure. It's one thing presenting a Thursday night Challenge Cup game in a warm studio, it's quite another to present England v South Africa from the touch-line at Twickenham. It took a fair while for me to feel at all relaxed. And just a few months into the gig, the broadcasting gods must have got together and thought they'd test my mettle.

The venue was Adams Park in High Wycombe, then home to London Wasps. I always hated Adams Park. It sits in a valley, the ground is often frosty, it's a concrete block of a stadium, it's always windy, and the studio was positioned on a gantry right under a dirty great tannoy. Still, we'd had a really good broadcast down at Exeter the day before, where I'd begun to feel like I was finding my groove as lead presenter. A few gags, a bit of back and forth, some good debate, and I was starting to stretch my legs out beneath the desk.

The build-up for Wasps v Bath began at 1.30 p.m., for a 1.45 kick-off. And because it wasn't much of a build-up and it was a Sunday lunchtime, none of us were really concentrating. I remember the PA saying, 'OK everyone, we're on air in two minutes', and my exact thought was 'Jesus, I'm simply not ready for this.' I hadn't done much prep, I hadn't got my levels right in my audio mix, I couldn't really hear anything, I hadn't really worked out what I was going to say and it suddenly hit me that I didn't have time to sort things out.

When we went on air, I had the added distraction of the tannoy blasting out announcements, and my voice was coming back into my headphones on a half-second delay, which has the effect of jamming your brain. In the panic of not knowing what to say I attempted the most convoluted, complicated tongue-twister of an opening link. Which didn't work. So I tried again. And it got worse. And I had another run-up, but by now I wasn't even speaking English.

Words were coming out in fits and starts – some too slow, some too long, some in the wrong order – and the agony went on for 20 seconds, although it seemed like time had stopped. Eventually my producer said, 'Stop talking and just introduce your guests,' so I asked for the viewers' forgiveness and brought in Ieuan Evans, Dean Ryan and Will Greenwood, who all managed to combine a look of stunned confusion and wild amusement. They actually did extremely well not to burst out laughing.

For years, I'd been trying to bury my imposter syndrome, thinking I didn't really deserve to be there, and now it felt as if I'd been unmasked as the total incompetent I really was, live on air. I wasn't a proper trained journalist, I was just a fan who'd got lucky. It was the most almighty brain fart, and I couldn't really see the funny side at first, although I did post something on Twitter as soon as the broadcast was over, asking if anyone could teach me to speak English. Thankfully, Twitter wasn't the toxic cesspit it would become, but even though everyone was very good about it (the producer acknowledged it was a bad one, but also said not to worry), I was bowled all ends up.

I came home that evening, and my wife and sister were in the kitchen. My wife asked how the show had gone, and I replied, 'I've had a really, really bad day.' 'You always say that,' she said, 'I'm sure it was absolutely fine.' 'No,' I replied, 'it was absolutely terrible.' I'd recorded it on the Sky box, and when I showed her, she paused, couldn't make eye contact and quietly said, 'Yeah, I can see what you mean.'

To make matters worse, while the player interview feature I'd spent much of the week lovingly putting together had got about 12,000 views online, a clip of my Adams Park implosion got half a million views in its first afternoon on YouTube, which just goes to show; if you're looking for an audience, do things badly.

The following week, I was in Belfast for a European Cup game and I was terrified. In my head, the whole country tuned in – families gathered around their TVs munching popcorn, drinkers glued to screens in pubs, crowds watching in the window of Dixons, everyone willing me to have another apparent stroke – and I was worried that if I suffered two almighty brain farts in a row, they might start thinking, *Hmmm, not sure this is working …* I don't think I've ever felt nerves again like the ten seconds before we went on air that night, but I mumbled my way through and managed to get away with it.

As bad as that meltdown was, and as much as I tortured myself over it, I've come to think that it was one of the best things that happened to me career-wise. It eventually helped me take the pressure off – no one had died and the sun came up the following morning. In a funny way, it lowered the tightrope for the rest of my career. I never took things as seriously after that. Why beat myself up over mistakes that hurt nobody when I could just carry on enjoying what I was doing for as long as I could?

I also had to remind myself that while 90 per cent of the public thought that sports broadcasting was a walk in the park – 'How hard can chatting about rugby be?' – they only thought that because there are some very good sports broadcasters out there.

During one Lions tour, my sound engineer wrote down all of the people I am listening to and taking direction from while fronting a live broadcast, and it added up to 17. When I'm talking into my microphone, I can have the director telling me what pictures he's going to float in, at the same time as the producer is telling me who I need to link to next, at the same time as the PA is telling me how long I need to be talking for, at the same time as I'm trying to think of a question to ask the four guests alongside. Throw in reporters in the tunnel and commentators on the gantry, production crew clipping up footage, floor managers moving us around, sound engineers fiddling with our levels and statisticians feeding in relevant data, and it can get pretty busy on the airwaves. And that's before you've added 80,000 spectators, fireworks, rain, and in-stadium entertainment. It's not brain surgery, far from it, but on the biggest days it's a hell of a buzz.

I recently presented a triathlon event in San Francisco with a guy who had created thousands of hours of content, but none of it live. I could tell he was quite nervous when he arrived in the studio, and when I sent him a thank you message after the broadcast, he replied, 'I had no concept of what a live broadcast was like, my appreciation of your craft has gone up massively.'

I'm certainly not trying to make out that live broadcasting is as challenging as hostage negotiation or underwater welding, but it is definitely not for everyone. The wonder isn't that presenters occasionally have meltdowns, it's that they don't happen more. And when I hear people criticising sports presenters for not asking follow-up questions, or fluffing a link, or fumbling a line, I think, *Yeah, you're probably right, but I'd love to give you the opportunity to show us how it should be done.* I'm amazed, in 2025, that no one's come up with the show *Trolls on TV*, where keyboard warriors get hauled out of their bedrooms in their Y-fronts and are put on live TV to show the world how they can do it better. 'Who was better? Voting lines are open ...'

Being live on air can also be a hair-raising experience for guests, even without all those voices in their ears. I'll never forget presenting the 2013 Heineken Cup final between Toulon and Clermont in Dublin, when we had Munster, Ireland and Lions legend Ronan O'Gara as a studio pundit for the first time. Here was a man who had won two Heineken Cups and a Grand Slam, but two minutes before we went on air he leant over and admitted he wasn't sure he could do the show. He was so jittery that I honestly thought he might pull out, but part of my role was to assure him that once he'd got his first answer out of the way, he'd relax. Thankfully, he did, and he's grown into one of the most polished and authoritative voices in the game. He was the star of the show in our Lions coverage of 2025 with his insights and sharp sense of humour. He keeps his presenters on their toes.

Presenters use what we call open talkback, which means anyone can talk to me at any time, but if someone wants to talk to the guests, they have to press a button, and normally only producers and directors do that. Having said that, things can still go horribly wrong for guests, like the time Hask had his famous meltdown at Twickenham in 2018.

Hask was standing with Will Greenwood pitchside while I was in the studio, and when I asked how the England team, who had just beaten South Africa, would celebrate their win, he said they'd be 'having a shing-shong'.

There followed ten more seconds of slurred gobbledy-gook before Will finally stepped in. Viewers thought Hask was drunk or on drugs, and the clip instantly went viral on social media. In fact, everything he was saying was repeating in his earpiece a couple of seconds later, which, as I knew only too well, was extremely off-putting. Most people would have said, 'I'm so sorry, I can't really hear properly,' but Hask carried on playing while the ship was sinking and was almost underwater by the time Will threw back to me.

I love the fact that he and I have the same battle scar, and I also love the fact that it's one of two things Hask is primarily remembered for, along with running into a post against Wales. All that glory in his career boiled down into two memes. The cherry on top of his broadcasting debacle was, for some unknown reason, him pretending to be the groundsman mowing the pitch as we said goodbye and went off air. I don't know whose idea that was and I don't know how it came about, but it didn't work for anybody on any level. I think that was the last time he was employed by a mainstream broadcaster.

I should also mention that a few years after my meltdown, I got a call from a production company which was putting together a rugby bloopers talking heads show. They wanted to include my brain fart, and said they'd pay me £500 to broadcast it in perpetuity. I said no, and kept saying no, but they eventually ground me down and I went and did an interview about it. Every Christmas when that show gets rolled out, I receive a flurry of messages along the lines of, 'You're not very good on TV.' The one consolation is that Hask's meltdown is two places ahead of mine at number one.

Thankfully, my misstep in Dublin a few years later didn't make the blooper video cut. It was a freezing cold day, I was talking through some graphics at the end of the game, and when I took a step backwards I disappeared off our broadcasting platform. My guest, former Ireland and Lions winger Luke Fitzgerald, managed to catch me, thus saving me from total ignominy, but it was another reminder that you can do thousands of hours of live television with hardly anyone noticing but cock one thing up and end up all over social media.

But the older I've got, the more I've grown to love those moments, the little windows into just how seat of-the-pants and high-risk live TV is. I've built up quite a showreel of shockers and picked up plenty of presenting scars, and I wouldn't send any of them back.

Mistakes were a big part of why legendary BBC broadcasters David Coleman and Murray Walker were so popular. Yes, they were mostly brilliant at what they did, but their occasional slips made them more human and relatable. Nowadays, I quite enjoy the challenge of trying to extricate myself from sticky situations – and I end up in quite a lot of those broadcasting alongside Tins and Hask – rather than just lobbing easy questions. I have gone from being terrified of going off-script to relishing the moments of drama and unpredictability. Broadcasting is at its most fun when it all goes wrong.

Mind you, there's stuff going wrong on air and there's almost not getting on air at all, which is another level of disaster entirely. I'd only been presenting for about 12 months when I was booked to do some corporate hospitality on an England match day at Twickenham – 'Hello, welcome, here's what's in store today. Have a lovely lunch, please buy some raffle tickets,' that sort of thing. The match finished at 5 p.m., I had to do a few bits afterwards, like interview a couple of players in the room, and then I had to hotfoot it to Sky Sports HQ in Isleworth by 7, to present our weekly highlights show. It was all easily doable, I'd parked in the right place and was in total control. Until they closed the car park for 70 minutes after the game to let the spectators get away.

By the time I finally escaped the carpark, I was 15 minutes away and was on air in ten minutes. I was almost in tears as I drove at breakneck speed through the backstreets of West London, contemplating my career going up in smoke – it's not a great look when a programme goes on air and the presenter isn't in his seat – but I somehow managed to be in place as the opening titles were rolling, smelling of burnt clutch and burnt rubber.

My heart was going ten to the dozen, my co-presenter James Gemmell was mildly amused about my hyper-panic and bailed me out. As we came on air, it suddenly occurred to me that I hadn't seen a minute of the rugby we'd be talking about. It was the broadcasting equivalent of missing the team bus and turning up late without your boots.

As it turned out, it was one of the most enjoyable shows I'd ever done. Because I was so relieved and euphoric about the fact that I'd salvaged my career, the two hours just flew by. My producer was very good about it. When we went off air, he said something like, 'I think we got away with it, we'll keep this between us,' and so much of television is fly by the seat of your pants. There's a lot of making things up on the hoof, holding things together with Sellotape, closing your eyes and driving through the fire. Having said that, they don't really expect their presenters to light the fire and then chuck petrol on it.

16

STRETCHERED OFF AT TWICKENHAM

TINS

Whenever I'm asked about my worst performances on a rugby field, the one that always springs to mind is England's final pool game against Scotland at the 2011 World Cup.

I was on medication for a tooth infection, and it had given me the shits and sapped me of any energy. I couldn't even warm up, and that continued into the game. Before kick-off, Chris Ashton had said to me, 'Thom Evans is going to use his left-hand fend, just make sure you chop him down,' but the first time Thom got the ball, I missed him and Ashy gave me a bollocking. I lasted 70 minutes and we ended up winning 16–12 (courtesy of a late try by Ashton), but I hadn't had much impact on the game.

However badly I played, I always believed that I'd play well next time, although I couldn't argue when Johnno (head coach Martin Johnson) told me I wasn't playing in the quarter-finals. It's probably the only time in my career I wish I had backed myself and told Johnno I would sort it in the next game and give me that chance. Instead I watched the game from the stands, we conceded a couple of tries I thought if I was on the field might not have happened but that's sport and we were out of the RWC. I was 33 by then but obviously still learning. I should have stood up for myself more, even if it didn't change Johnno's mind.

When I was at Bath, I got norovirus, which meant I was unable to eat and basically spent seven days on the toilet. But because we were in a battle at the wrong end of the table, (head coach) Brian Smith said he needed me to play at the weekend. I told him that I didn't think I'd last, and he replied that he just needed me for that one game, and that I wouldn't have to play on the following Wednesday. I didn't play particularly well, but having got through 60 minutes and emptied the tank, Brian said, 'I need you to go again on Wednesday …' I did as I was told and was awful.

Fans watch a game, see someone play badly and conclude that they're suddenly not very good. They have no idea what's going on behind the scenes, which is tough, because bad performances can damage a player's reputation. And I did find it amazing when a coach asked me to play when I didn't feel right, I played badly, and then I would have to face the music. I'd think, *You could have played someone who was fit, full of energy and enthusiastic and they'd have done a better job*. But it takes a strong character to stick to your guns and say to a coach outright, 'I'm not playing this week,' and my persona was all about fronting up for the team and my coaches, sometimes with disastrous results.

In 2009, Gloucester played Ospreys in the semi-finals of the Anglo-Welsh Cup, and I told (head coach) Dean Ryan that I wasn't fit. Dean said he needed me, I suffered a knee injury that put me out for the rest of the season. Coaches need to understand a player's personality, so that if he goes to the well for you every time he plays, they've got to trust him on the rare occasions he says he doesn't feel right. Then again, I did play games when I felt rough or not quite right physically and had a blinder, so it's not an exact science.

To be fair, I think most people accepted that I needed some time off after England's Six Nations game against Wales in 2008. We were winning when I went to dive on the ball and Lee Byrne got in ahead of me, and as he fly-hacked the ball ahead, he caught me in the ribs with his trailing foot.

The physio knew I was in a lot of pain because we had a deal: if I was rolling around on the floor, I was hurt but probably all right; but if I was lying still in a foetal position, it was something serious. And on this occasion, I'd barely moved an inch. When he ran on, he asked what was wrong, and I said I thought I'd broken some ribs. When he asked if I could get to my feet, I said I didn't think I could. He then said he'd ask for a stretcher, to which I replied, 'I'm not getting stretchered off at Twickenham.' Pasky (Phil Pask, the England physio) said to me, 'Get up then.' I managed to get on all fours, before immediately rolling back into the foetal position and saying, 'Get me the stretcher.'

When Zara came into the medical room, she asked what was wrong with me. I told her I thought I'd broken some ribs, and she replied, 'Oh, that's OK, then.' You've got to remember that Zara's sport of eventing is even more dangerous than rugby, and we always use humour to get through difficult times. However, I had a feeling that it was more than just broken ribs, because when I took a deep breath, it wouldn't end.

When I turned up at the hospital, the surgeon said to me, 'I don't know why you're here. You've clearly just broken your ribs, it seems to be a bit of a waste of time.' The morphine was kicking in and I was feeling quite relaxed, so instead of arguing with the guy, I said, 'OK, if that's what you think ...' Thirty minutes later, he returned looking white as a ghost. 'We need to get you into intensive care immediately,' he said. 'You've got a punctured lung and a tear in your liver.' Apparently, blood was pooling into the sac around my liver and if that burst, it was bad news.

Next thing I knew, I was in intensive care with lines going into my neck, surrounded by dying people. It felt like the most miserable place on the planet. I was in there for three or four days, and fortunately the sac didn't burst.

The sports reporter Ian Stafford discovered the extent of my injuries and went a bit wilder than I would have wanted – the headline suggested I was on the brink of death – but it was quite a bad injury. Thank God the England medical team had decided to send me to hospital, otherwise things might have turned out quite badly. Who knows what might have happened if I'd taken some painkillers and had a beer with the team.

At the same time, once I was in intensive care, I always felt they were on top of things, and I never thought I was at death's door. My main goal was removing that line going into my neck and going home as soon as possible. Physios had always commented on how quickly and well I healed, and I was back playing rugby six weeks later.

I can't recall how Johnno asked me to be England captain, or even where it happened, but I do remember that it was before our first game of the 2011 Six Nations, against Wales in Cardiff, and Moodos (the official captain Lewis Moody) was still coming back from injury.

We won that game against the Welsh, before beating Italy and France, but I then ruptured ankle ligaments against Scotland. It was still a nice occasion because Princess Anne, who's the patron of Scottish Rugby as well as being my mother-in-law, had to present me with the Calcutta Cup. I said to her, 'Shall we have a debrief over lunch tomorrow,' to which she replied, 'Move on, Michael.'

Luckily, some bone had snapped off with the ligament, which made it easier to graft back into place and recover from.

I've always been very proud to be English and love belting out the anthem before a game. I understand that English history isn't perceived as all great, but I think we're far too apologetic nowadays. We led the world in so many ways and should be proud of our achievements, while learning from our mistakes.

The other home nations don't really hate us, but when it comes to sport, it works for them to pretend they do. By harking back to conflicts they had with us in the past, it stirs certain emotions and gives them an edge on a rugby field. They also accuse England of being arrogant, although I don't think we are. We're a far bigger country than Wales, Scotland and Ireland, with more rugby clubs, a larger player pool and more money, so England fans thinking we should be more dominant than we are, isn't arrogance, it's just logic.

Of course, it's not just the home nations who think we're arrogant and claim to hate us. And I certainly get the feeling that while South Africa like to hate everyone when it comes to rugby, they like to hate England the most.

Since the Springboks returned from the international wilderness in 1992, games between us and them have tended to be feisty affairs, full of claret and broken bones, and not much focus on shape.

England's tour of South Africa in 1994 was brutal, with a host of England players suffering injuries, including Jon Callard, who almost lost an eye when his head was stamped on in a game against Eastern Province, and the game between England and the Springboks at Twickenham in 1997 was carnage.

My first Test against South Africa was in Pretoria in 2000, and I believe that was the first time a TMO was ever used in international rugby. We thought Tim Stimpson had won the game for us, but the referee went upstairs, the TMO was South African, and funnily enough he disallowed the try. We did manage to square the series in Bloemfontein, but it was another ill-tempered affair.

I've already written about our game against the Boks in 2002, when Robbie Fleck and his team-mates completely lost the plot, and that's almost what was expected of England–South Africa matches back then. The Boks are always big lads and they're going to try to stamp all over you. If you don't win the physical contest against them, you have no chance of winning the game. And while I always enjoyed that challenge, it's easier said than done, especially against the team they've got now.

17

TURNING 40

HASK

A lot has gone on since the last book we wrote, including me turning 40. I celebrated with a mad week in Ibiza, which was like a cross between *The Hangover* and the last days of Rome. Some people broke so hard that they felt the need to leave early. I'd wake up and see a note next to my bed – 'Sorry can't do this anymore.'

This one lad had been out for two days straight. No sleep, no pause, just clubs, basements and borrowed cigarettes. When he finally staggered home, he wasn't alone. Trailing behind him was a girl from Venezuela, the kind of beauty that makes the room tilt slightly when she smiles. Their entire romance was conducted through Google Translate on his phone: stilted sentences, broken words, and laughter filling in the gaps. Communication: difficult, but not impossible.

We had a club room in the house, so naturally he took her there. Things were going well until he decided the moment needed a little powder. He laid out what he thought was cocaine, took a heroic bump, and instantly realised something was wrong. It wasn't cocaine. It was ketamine.

Panic set in. His logic, if you can call it that, was to fix the mistake with more cocaine. So he racked up an even bigger line, threw it down his nose, and felt the world cave in again. It wasn't cocaine this time either. Another mountain of ketamine.

Within minutes he'd gone full K-hole. While he sat, paralysed in the chair, the Venezuelan girl danced around to music only she could hear. Somehow – and this part I'll never understand – he clawed his way back to functioning, at least enough to have sex with her. But halfway through, she suddenly turned her head, looked into the empty corner of the room, and waved cheerfully at … nothing.

He froze. She wasn't waving at him. She was waving at someone or something that simply wasn't there. That was the moment he shattered.

By morning it was his birthday, though you wouldn't have known it. He came downstairs wrapped in a duvet like a ghost, muttering to himself. He reminded me of Martin Sheen's Captain Willard in *Apocalypse Now*, after a few hours in the company of Colonel Kurtz. I watched him sit with his laptop for four hours, staring, clicking, achieving nothing. Then he put it away, produced someone else's laptop, and repeated the ritual. At one point we had to confiscate the shoelaces and belts, so convinced were we that he might simply decide to check out of life altogether.

Every demon he'd ever suppressed seemed to crawl out of the woodwork that day. Every half-finished plan, every mistake, every failure sat on his shoulders. He folded in on himself, a man imploding on his own birthday. He claimed he looked into hell and all the light and fun drained from the world. Eventually, I had to phone his brother to get him to have a word and talk him off the ledge. Every time he had gone up to his room we were worried he was going to throw himself off.

Another mate sat me down and said, 'All for one and one for all. I'll be here until the bitter end.'

One night, one of the lads got really deep about the meaning of true friendship and how he'd never let me down, and that I needed to keep good people around me. We all went to bed and when I woke up the next day, I went to find my reliable and trusted friend only to discover he had got up early and caught a flight home. He messaged me the following morning: 'Sorry mate, broken.'

I wanted to have a trip that was focused on hanging around with the guys, chatting shit, rather than partying and trying to chat up women. There were big lunches every day, with lots of drinks, and I don't think I've spoken so much nonsense in my entire life. And I've got a very high bar. Turning 40 wasn't at all depressing, it was non-stop laughter, exactly what I wanted.

Physically, I'm a strange mismatch between outwardly looking half-decent and crumbling underneath. I've had a bit of a mid-life glow-up – lid done, teeth done – and I reckon I might even be a six out of ten. I also went from 123 kg (19 st 5 lb) to 107 kg (16 st 12 lb), having linked up with Roar Fitness, which is run by former British speed skater Sarah Lindsay. They provided personal training at a reduced rate in exchange for me promoting them on my social media, including a photoshoot. I didn't need to do it, I just loved the torture of doing it, and it was the best shape I'd ever been in. I was absolutely shredded and looked almost like a bodybuilder, minus the severe bronze lacquer. I mean I did get tanned – just not that insane tan they all get.

Someone recently pointed out that I'm always saying, 'I *have* to do this, then I *have* to do that', and when I say that, I mean it literally. I had a quiet period recently and hated it. I got really bored and very irritable, which is why I *have* to work. And while not working means I can at least make music and scribble ideas down, as well as spend quality time with my daughter, I also end up wasting an enormous amount of time and money dating.

I've never really been a fan of dating apps. I much prefer meeting people in person. There's an art to chatting someone up, that mix of charm, nerves and risk. I actually enjoy the jeopardy of it: that little thrill of not knowing whether they'll say yes, no, or completely shut you down. I enjoy the process of trying to refine your skills, and just when you think you have it nailed, someone just laughs in your face and walks off. Or maybe that's just me.

What always makes me laugh is how often women complain that men don't approach them, as if it's the easiest thing in the world. They don't quite realise just how nerve-wracking it is. Most women never hit on men, so they'll never know the feeling of walking up to a group, heart pounding, trying to deliver a line that isn't terrible. Sometimes it lands, sometimes it crashes and burns and either way, it takes guts.

I did once try to get onto Raya, the so-called 'celebrity' dating app, though whether it's A-list or Z-list is up for debate. After 97 referrals, I still couldn't get in. I've no idea what I did wrong, but perhaps they're simply excellent judges of character. It's probably for the best that they've kept me out.

The problem is, most of the time I date just to have something to do, and it can be quite soul-destroying. I always feel like I should pay, because it's the old-school gentlemanly thing to do and the way I was brought up, and I have always been that way. Most don't offer anyway, and if I did suggest we split the bill (which I never would) they'd probably tell everyone what a tight bastard I was. But what irritates me more is that some women don't even say thank you for anything let alone dinner. I'll watch them climb into a cab and think, 'That is not a good person. What a complete waste of time and money.'

I've got no intention of settling down with anybody anytime soon, if I am completely honest, and I've pretty much conceded that my life needs to be slightly chaotic. But what that chaos will look like over the next few years is difficult to say. For probably the first time in my life, I'm not really sure what the hell I'm supposed to be doing.

Having joined a new management agency with a plan to build something long-term, career wise, things didn't work out, so I'm without management at the time of writing. Music-wise, I've rebranded as 'HASKELL', and have worked with some amazing labels, but it hasn't led to big traction and money quite yet. I have been on a hell of a journey and lots of things I have done I was never sure I would ever do, but my mentality is you always want more and always want to do better. Music, it's still a big passion, but it's not progressing as quickly as I'd like. I think if I was younger then it wouldn't be a problem or there would not be as much pressure for it to happen now, but I am not 22 starting out, I am 40 going into a career that while you can do it at any age, a lot of the artists who are doing well, really resonate with a younger audience. Now, while I feel 21 in my mind, bits are falling off me, I'm like one of those old transformers from the movie series of the same name, who as they walk along nuts, bolts and limbs just fall off.

A lot of people still have no idea that I make music and travel the world performing. In a week's time I will be releasing my 28th recording which is insane to me. It's my first solo release on Toolroom. I actually got back from the Burning Man festival two days before I went to Dubrovnik and while I was there, I went to watch Carl Cox play, who again is a mate and mentor and the king of dance music. I had been there for 20 minutes, dancing and taking it all in, when I was talking to my Aussie mate Heath, and I interrupted him to say, 'That's my track!' He said 'What?' I said, 'That's my track, Carl is playing my track!' Carl Cox was playing my unreleased track 'Shake That', in front of 2,000 people. It was insane. I was so excited, I went right to the front and caught Carl's eye and we had this moment, it was amazing. I have it all on video as well. It's stuff like that, which makes you want to keep on playing. There are amazing people like Mark and Carl who have helped me so much, that I can't repay them.

I am not going to give up anytime soon, I have this hunger to travel and play around the world, and it will happen, I absolutely 100 per cent believe that. I have lots of music to get signed and I am launching my own label very soon, which will again change the game for me. I have the same hunger for DJing as I did for playing rugby, and that turned out OK. One of the hardest parts of this is building a new audience. Those of you reading this book probably don't really care about my music, nor does a lot of my social media audience; they came to me because I was a rugby player not a musician. Hence why I rebranded, to disassociate from James Haskell, the Z-list celeb and sportsperson.

I truly believe when you have found something that you love, you have to pursue it. Life is too short not to follow your passions. I know a lot of unhappy people wishing they were doing something else. I am lucky to have found DJing, as I have the most fun doing it.

What can make things better is if the gigs are wicked, the crowd engaged and I get to play the music I want. However, even though I have been playing for a number of years, 12 now, I often end up playing gigs that don't make much sense and the music I have to play is not what I enjoy. I also often follow on from a DJ who doesn't know how to warm-up a crowd properly. Imagine coming to play a set and the guy is playing 138 drum and bass, when you are a tech house DJ. Or you are headlining a club and the guy is playing a techno ABBA remix. I always look at the slot I am playing and who is around me, and think about having some moments in my set but making sure I don't play too hard, to pick a style that suits the crowd but matches the other artists on the line-up and stay in my lane. Then, before the next DJ comes on, I will take the energy down a bit to give him room to play. Or I will echo my track out and they can start afresh. A lot of the time I come on and I am like 'Jesus, what the hell do I do with this?' DJing is not about mental transitions, it's about picking the right music for the crowd at the right time, and getting people dancing. I spend most of my set looking at who is dancing and what kind of thing they want, which is often very hard in mixed crowds because almost all of them want something different.

One of my biggest bugbears is when events, especially these health and wellness festivals, put no thought into the line-ups and how they structure the events and running order for the music. At one gig, after driving for six hours, I went on after a folk group at lunchtime, and my audience was a few crazy middle-aged women with pink hair and crystals stuck to their faces. I was happy to play and got people dancing, but it was kind of pointless. As I was packing up my gear, what appeared to be a very large family dressed in 18th-century clothes and holding ancient instruments filed out of a green camper van parked next to my car. They were next on the bill. If you use the analogy of baking a cake, it's like you start with flour, then add some calamari, then some custard, then a lamb chop – it makes no sense, nothing goes with anything else, no one can flow with the vibe. You have people who love folk, but hate dance, then you have dance people who don't want to hear an indie band moaning and wailing about how shit life is. I remember I did Car Fest, which was amazing but they put me on after an American rock band, then had the Rick Parfitt Jnr band on after me. From rock, to dance, to pop, then it was Rick Astley and then Craig David. Mental.

During the Welsh gig my brother slept in the car instead of watching my set – that's what you call commitment to the cause. I often take someone with me to gigs, it's normally Kallum, my video guy (yes, his name starts with a 'K', fuck knows why, it's like his mum wanted his life to be slightly harder than it needed to be). We arrived back in London around one in the morning. The next day I picked up Bodhi at around 8 a.m., had her until 5 p.m., drove to Exmouth and DJ'ed at a beach party. Which was a vibe. The organisers had booked me into a three-star shitbox of a hotel – hot as an oven, didn't even have any Scottish shortbread or a Corby trouser press, and you could still see a faint chalk outline where someone had died and the shower you knew would definitely give you Legionnaires' disease – so I decided to drive home instead. Which was the least smart thing I have done in a while. The first two hours were fine, I was buzzing from the gig, adrenaline was high. Then I became tired, like so tired that I was never going to make it. I stopped and thought about having a sleep but I knew I would not get up again if I did, so I got a coffee, a Red Bull and some water. I also had a couple of sniffs of smelling salts that my mate had given me, they were Eddie Hall ones, so they were fucking nuclear, I did one large inhale and my soul left my body. Somehow I got home safe and sound, and went to bed, but the lesson was learned: it is better to stay in a hotel that resembles downtown Mogadishu than to try and drive home late at night.

* * *

Then there was Glastonbury, which was absolute insanity. I wasn't meant to be DJing, but I ended up doing four sets. When I turned up, I was standing in the queue for a shuttle bus and started chatting to four girls dressed in matching gold outfits. 'Off to anywhere nice?' I asked them. 'Yep, we're going to a special party.' 'Oh, I quite like special parties. How special is it?' 'Very special. Not for you.' 'I'm sure I could get in if I wanted to.' 'No, it's definitely not for you.' Well, it didn't exactly turn out like that.

No sooner had I checked into our glamping tent than I'd received a message asking me to DJ at a party. I had a couple of drinks, watched Josh Baker and Radio 1's Danny Howard play, then looked at where I was meant to be playing. Glastonbury is fantastic, but it's endless. I've been a few times now and never seen or been anywhere near some of the areas. People are always asking where you are, to which the reply is usually, 'I have no idea!' You also have no phone signal so you can't really get through to people which makes meeting up really tricky. I try not to ever lose the group I am with as it can take hours to find each other again.

The party that I had been asked to DJ at the last minute was at the other end of the site apparently, and appeared to be a house in the grounds of Glastonbury, which made no real sense but we rolled with it. To make matters worse, I've got arthritis in my ankle, which means I hobble, and Tom, the friend who I had come with, has had a fused ankle and was carrying a staff like Gandalf, which was apt, because finding this place was like a mission from *The Lord of the Rings*.

After what seemed like hours – and probably was hours, come to think of it – we finally reached our destination, which did turn out to be an actual house beyond the festival fence but inside the outer fence, hidden by bushes. There was a free bar, a DJ tent, Seb Fontaine was playing – and everyone was dressed in gold. After making enquiries, I discovered that three investment bankers rented the house from site owner and festival founder Michael Eavis every year, for some insanely low sum, just so they could have this one party and get VIP tickets to the festival. It was the perfect crime, and I was very jealous. The old farmhouse and garden were magical and you would never know it was even there. I think it's fair to say that modern-day Glastonbury has drifted somewhat from its hippie roots.

The first people I saw at the bar were the four girls I'd met in the queue for a shuttle bus. 'Fucking hell girls, turns out it's not that much of a secret party is it,' I said. 'How did you get in?' 'Believe it or not, I'm your DJ!' 'What?' 'Yep, you're welcome.' The lads who were renting the house were awesome and managed to get ten of my mates in, Seb smashed his set, then Carly Wilford killed hers with some mega tunes and I kept everyone vibing during mine. It was a really nice touch to have a wicked crowd ready to dance and all my mates watching me play my first set at Glasto. Once I was done DJing, it thought it was time to party so me, Tom and his wife Arabella got written off with my mates and partied until the early hours. It was a big start, but bear in mind it was just Thursday, with three more nuclear days to go.

We went pretty hard on Friday, and on Saturday morning, due to a diary oversight, I had a long drive to Norwich to play a festival. As is my wont, I had to listen to '80s power ballads to keep myself from nodding off or descending into despair, having left my friends. When you go into the cauldron of Glasto, bonds are formed, and I was getting PTSD every hour that I was away from them. The '80s music kept me in a positive mood, and a bit like Alan Partridge enjoys his car bangers, I was enjoying mine.

On arrival in Norwich, I discovered that Professor Green, who was meant to be headlining, had pulled out, so I had to play for longer. And once I was done, I drove all the way back to Glasto. When I was reunited with my friends Tom and Arabella, it was like I'd been suffering from separation anxiety, because I was just so glad to see them.

Having partied all through the night, I got invited to DJ at Soho House's pop-up venue, where I turned the VIP area into a full-on rave. It was wicked fun, and some of my mates had hovered into view again so the vibes and spirits were high on a tricky day at Glastonbury. I'd just finished up there when someone messaged me to say someone had dropped out elsewhere and could I come and play later on that evening. I said yes in a heartbeat because that would be my first proper Glasto gig, as in on an official stage. The first two sets had been at Winding Lake, the VIP glamping area where we stayed, and they had been really fun as they were a couple of morning sets, to get people back vibing before they headed back in for another day of carnage.

However, it meant I had to leave The Prodigy performance halfway through, which my mates weren't particularly thrilled about because they were absolutely sensational. 'Listen,' I said, 'everyone relax, you don't have to come and watch me, I'm going to do it anyway.' I agreed to do it so I had to do. Being good mates, they wanted to support me, so said they would all come on the epic adventure.

Now picture the scene: Glastonbury, the holy land of music, mud and questionable decision-making. I'd agreed to do the DJ set – nothing unusual there – but what I hadn't realised until about an hour before was that the stage I was playing on was approximately three postal codes away from The Prodigy on the Other Stage. Basically, if you wanted to get there, you needed a sherpa, a camel, and perhaps a letter of recommendation from Bear Grylls. Not ideal when one's limbs are creaking with arthritis and the ground is already ankle-deep in piss.

So off we went, my merry band of lunatics, when I made what can only be described as a catastrophic error. One of my mates was nibbling on a chocolate bar. Being the prankster that I am, and not having eaten for hours, I snatched it straight from his hand and wolfed it down like Augustus Gloop. Only later did I discover it wasn't Dairy Milk – oh no, it was a bar of mushroom chocolate. Half a bar, gone, before the words 'don't eat that, you bell-end' had even hit the air.

Keith Flint may be gone, but 'Firestarter' was still alive in my bloodstream. I glanced at my friend Tom, who with his wizard's staff began to morph into a giant praying mantis. He leaned in close like one of the caricatures from the three brothers in the animated sequence in the movie *Harry Potter and the Deathly Hallows*, whispering absolute nonsense in my face, until I finally cracked up with laughter and said: 'Tom, for the love of God, please fuck off.'

Meanwhile his wife was skipping around in a pink tutu – that's right, an actual pink tutu, I wasn't hallucinating that bit – and every time she spoke, me and Mantis-Tom fell about laughing like children who'd just sniffed glue. Honestly, it was less 'professional DJ set incoming' and more 'Monty Python takes acid in a Somerset field'.

Now, ordinarily I'm the sober one. Rock solid. Never touched mushrooms in my life, barring one tragic dabble with mushroom oil. But here I was, absolutely tripping balls, the ground moving under my feet like a conveyor belt in Willy Wonka's factory, trying to work out whether I could still remember how walking functioned. Spoiler: barely. I had literally forgotten how the floor worked.

Luckily, one of our crew was a seasoned drugnaut, and they calmly fed me fizzy drinks and Haribo like I was a Victorian child recovering from scarlet fever. Slowly, with many stops, detours and bursts of deranged giggling, we staggered into the tent where I was due to play. It wasn't one of the big-name tents, but frankly by that stage I'd have been delighted if it was just four cows and a tractor.

When we turned up we found ourselves in a virtually empty tent. The DJ, who was playing disco, looked like Mr Mistoffelees from Andrew Lloyd Webber's *Cats*, except she was wearing a Panama hat. Meanwhile, back at the Other Stage, The Prodigy were coming towards the end of one of the greatest sets in the festival's history, which my friends kept reminding me of.

Gallows humour soon took over, at least among my friends. 'Are you sure you're going to be able to get to the decks through that crowd?' I did seriously wonder if there had been some kind of mistake and someone had booked me by accident. That's not unheard of at Glasto, where communication isn't always the easiest.

Now, if all that wasn't enough, one of my so-called friends kept sidling up to me, whispering, 'Mate ... do we need to book a VIP table? How do we get into the booth?' 'I think you should call the artist liaison to help you get through the crowd.'

The booth! The booth! I looked around at the tent which, let's be clear, was emptier than Prince Andrew's Christmas card list and thought: *Darling, there isn't even a crowd, let alone a bloody VIP section.* Unless by 'VIP' you mean the two cider-soaked hippies in the corner and a Labrador.

I'll admit, on one level I was howling with laughter, because of the absurdity of it all. But on another level deep inside my fragile mushroom-riddled soul, I was quietly dying. And then, to pour salt into my already hallucinogenic wound, someone kept reminding me: 'Listen James, if you smash this set, mate, you could be on the Pyramid Stage next year; the world is your oyster!'

Oh, thanks very much, what a comfort. Here I was, drooling into a packet of Haribo, staring at Tom the praying mantis, and suddenly I'm being told Glastonbury's biggest stage is within my grasp if I can just nail a gig in a tent emptier than a Wetherspoons at 8 a.m.

At this point, one of my crew took me aside for a pep talk. The solemn face, the arm round the shoulder, the whole Rocky Balboa in the locker room routine. 'James, listen, are you sure you're ready? The crowd's gonna be massive ...'

And that's when the real madness set in. Because behind my eyes, it wasn't me anymore. I became that weird bloke from *Men in Black* – you know, the giant that is dead in the morgue at the start of the movie who is powered by a tiny alien in his skull. That was me. A little mushroomed-up alien in my own head, peering out of the windows of my eyes, frantically trying to steer the enormous bodysuit called James Haskell. 'Left hand to crossfader … no, no, that's a Haribo. Shit. Abort!'

So picture the scene: empty tent, no VIP, no Pyramid Stage, just me, my mushroom pilot, and a set of decks I wasn't entirely sure weren't made of melting plasticine.

Once Miss Mistoffelees had finished her set, it was my turn. Simple enough, you'd think: walk into the booth, plug in, play. But no. Not at Glastonbury. Not on mushrooms.

To reach the decks, I first had to shuffle through a gate round the back, and then crawl – *crawl!* – beneath what looked like a children's climbing frame built by feral elves. It was so low, only a borrower could have slipped through without grazing their dignity. My mushroom-addled mind simply couldn't process whether this obstacle course was real or a hallucination, so I had to draft in one of my friends to confirm that yes, I wasn't mad, and yes, the only way in was to crawl under the bloody stage like Gollum sneaking into Mordor.

So there I was, climbing under beams, emerging up through a hole like a subterranean mole, until I popped up right beneath the decks. And who should be waiting but Miss Mistoffelees herself – not, I regret to report, purring with delight at my arrival. I turned on the old Haskell charm, all winks and bonhomie, but she gave me the kind of frosty reception you'd expect from a supply teacher who's just caught you reading a porn mag between the covers of *Romeo and Juliet.*

The frost only thickened when I slotted in my USB, loaded up some Afro House, and took a hard right turn away from her disco vibes. A pivot so sharp you could've sliced bread with it. I assured her she'd played a 'lovely set' – to which she responded with a curt tip of her hat before wriggling, rather undignified, back under the barrier and vanishing like a cabaret phantom.

And then ... it was me. Alone. Mushrooms humming, crowd invisible (at first), hands trembling as I cued the first track. Afro House vocals poured out into the emptiness ... and then something magical happened. Like the Pied Piper, I drew them in. People drifted across from other stages, trickling in, filling the void. Within minutes, the tent was alive – the crowd bouncing, sweating, arms aloft. I'd somehow picked the exact peak time to unleash a set of vocal Afro House bangers, and it went from wasteland to a scene of utter carnage in no time at all.

There was only one issue: the mushrooms. The entire time, I was convinced someone was standing directly behind me. Every 30 seconds I'd whip my head round, expecting to see Tom the praying mantis, or Miss Mistoffelees with her disco wand, but there was no one. Just me, grinning like a lunatic, hallucinating shadows and steering the ship by sheer muscle memory.

But here's the kicker – despite it all, it was seamless. Glorious. I went in under the stage like a terrified borrower, and came out the other side as the Mushroom Messiah of Afro House.

Set done, crowd conquered, mushrooms still humming in the background it was time for 'refreshments'. Now, I must stress, I was in 'glamping'. And I use that term very loosely. Yes, there was a canvas tent. Yes, there was a double bed. And yes, there was a socket where you could charge an iPhone if you crouched at the right angle. But let's be honest it was more budget safari than boutique luxury.

So, when one of the lads suggested we nip back to his tent, I was expecting more of the same: muddy ground, wet wipes, and perhaps, if we were lucky, a warm crate of Red Stripe.

Instead, we found ourselves walking down a dimly lit alley between tents, illuminated by lanterns swinging gently like something out of Charles Dickens. The flap of canvas opened and, my God, suddenly we weren't in Glastonbury anymore. We were in bloody Narnia.

I swear on my arthritic knees, it was palatial. I mean, one minute I'm in a field in Somerset, the next I'm stepping into Buckingham ruddy Palace. The place went on for miles. Rugs on the walls, Bayeux tapestry casually hanging up like it had been nicked from the British Museum, deer heads, spears, shields, an actual anteroom. There was a chap in the corner knocking out Old Fashioneds as if he'd wandered in from the Savoy.

My mushroom-saturated brain simply could not cope. *Where am I? What am I seeing? How has Henry VIII's hunting lodge been air-dropped into Worthy Farm?* It was Bedouin chic meets French Renaissance meets *Game of Thrones*. And I was utterly fried.

To top it off, we were served lobster. Lobster! At Glastonbury! Alongside foie gras, cocktails and a swimming pool annexe. I swear there was an orangery. An orangery! I don't even know what an orangery is, but by Christ there was one.

At this point I lay down on the bed, and suddenly I was gone. I sank into the mattress like a Victorian ghost child, disappearing into another dimension. Everyone else was floating above me, chatting, eating, drinking, while I lay there thinking: *Am I still at Glastonbury? Have I stumbled into a portal? Am I perhaps back home in bed, or worse, am I in Norwich about to open for Professor Green?*

I'll never know the truth. But what I do know is that tent was the single biggest mindfuck of my life. A glamping tent that turned into Versailles. A field that turned into a palace. And me, lying there in a mushroom haze, not sure if I'd ever climb back out again.

Once we'd finally prised ourselves out of Versailles-in-a-tent – the only thing missing were concubines and a sacrificial altar (and between you and me, I knocked off a star on TripAdvisor for the lack of concubines) – we decided to squeeze the last drops out of Sunday before the hammer fell on Monday morning.

Now, technically, I was meant to be back for *GBR*. But Alex, in a moment of rare compassion, decided a car crash of a human being like me rocking up, sweating mushroom spores and speaking to imaginary praying mantises, was not what the podcast needed. So he stood me down. Glorious reprieve! That gave me licence to absolutely smash the arse out of my final Glasto night.

But here's the thing with Glastonbury: wherever you want to be, it's always on the other side of the moon. Everything is 'the arse end', because you're never where you need to be. We started walking, yomping, traipsing through the countryside like hobbits on the world's least organised quest. At some point, we gave up. Myself, Arabella and Tom peeled off, heading back to glamping. We'd missed the shuttle, of course, so it was yomping through hedgerows, country lanes, Google Maps telling us to walk into rivers, and demons appearing in the bushes.

At one stage I'm fairly certain I rode a dinosaur. Possibly a dragon. God knows what Tom was astride, but I didn't dare look as he was still terrifying, staff in hand like a cursed wizard. Somehow, we made it. Collapsed into our tents, gone.

Monday morning dawned, and I, being the foolhardy hero, volunteered to drive us back to London. An hour in, my eyelids were dropping like lead curtains. Arabella gamely took over, Tom was already unconscious, we'd had to fold him into the car like a deckchair. Within half an hour, I woke up to find the entire party asleep in a lay-by. Arabella had sensibly pulled over, bless her, but it felt like we'd been abducted by aliens. I rallied, filled myself with Red Bull, coffee, chewing gum, and gunned it back to London.

And because I have the organisational skills of a concussed ferret, I'd booked a DJ set that very night. Lady Wimbledon, the Wimbledon tennis launch party, in (you guessed it) Wimbledon. I stumbled into my house at 5.45, dropped my kit, showered, and was out the door by 6. Straight to the venue, straight to the decks.

But fate wasn't done with me. Before me on the line-up came a disgruntled, well, let's call her an 'ex', though in truth it was more a one-night cameo appearance. Regardless, she was not thrilled to see me. Evil eyes, cold shoulder, full passive-aggressive performance. And to top it off, she was banging out tech house at a volume better suited to Berghain in Berlin at 4 a.m. than a promotional soirée full of influencers nibbling canapés.

My turn came. I did what any seasoned pro does and I pivoted. Downshifted into Afro House, smoother, sexier, irresistible. Within minutes, the dancefloor was packed. The golden rule: get the girls dancing, the boys will follow. And follow they did. The place went off, influencers turning into sweaty ravers, Lady Wimbledon looking on like she'd discovered fire. Two hours, job done, dancefloor conquered.

I staggered into a car, got home, collapsed into bed … only to wake up the next morning and trot off to a live event with Alun Wyn Jones at O'Neill's for *GBR*. Why? Because my diary is a war crime, that's why.

So, one day I'm in the studio, the next I'm giving a speech at a Campion School old boys' dinner (which, let's be honest, is basically Hogwarts with port), the day after that I'm DJing at a rugby sevens festival in Wales where the rain was so biblical I half expected Noah to headline the second stage, and the day after that I've somehow agreed to DJ at this cool festival held at a brewery in Surrey. It was actually wicked, which made all the travel worth it. By Sunday I had my daughter and was on full Dad patrol, which was the most important gig of the weekend for me. Monday rolled round with the podcast, and then, naturally, I was off to Australia for the Lions series.

Frankly, it's like living in a Benny Hill sketch with an international flight schedule. But I do thrive on chaos. If my diary isn't trying to kill me, I don't feel like I'm moving forward.

Now, let's clear up one thing: if you thought my Glasto weekend sounded lucrative, think again. Every single set was free. Not a penny. The only fee I received was a year's free membership to Soho House, which, while very civilised, doesn't pay for flights or nappies. (Although it does give you access to overpriced negronis and conversations with men called Tarquin who 'dabble in crypto', so it's swings and roundabouts, every cloud and all that.)

Some gigs do pay, and pay well, but not all of them are exactly my vibe, to put it mildly. The rugby sevens festival was … jolly. Rain hammering down, everyone in ponchos, and me obliged to play the holy trinity of 'Show Me Love', 'Music Sounds Better With You' and whatever else you'd hear at a wedding just before the buffet opens. Lovely tunes, obviously, but for me it's like being asked to perform Shakespeare and instead reading the Argos catalogue.

Elemental Festival, however, now that was my jam. That was the Sunday gig at the brewery in Surrey, the crowd properly up for it, me playing exactly what I wanted. It reminded me why I fell in love with DJing in the first place. No requests for Ed Sheeran. No soggy rugby fans. Just pure, unfiltered music and sweaty people going absolutely barmy.

And the releases? Oh, I've been busier than a Tory MP deleting WhatsApps. New records every month since

January 2025. It's a crowded market: there are more tech house tracks out there than there are oat milk brands in Shoreditch, but here's the kicker: big names are playing my stuff. At Glasto, Skepta, Mochakk and Carlita did a back-to-back-to-back, and right in the middle of their set, one of my tracks called 'Go Deep' went off. I nearly fell over. Proper global stars, playing my music, in front of thousands. And Marco Carola also played my track 'Check It Out' at one of his events! Which, in DJ terms, is like having the Pope slip one of your demos into Sunday Mass.

So yes, I can read a crowd now, I'm a decent technical DJ, and I'm convinced that if I hadn't been a public-schoolboy rugby player, I might have been a bit further along. But sod it I'm here, I'm still standing, and clearly I'm doing something right if the heavyweights are giving my tracks a spin. All I want now is to travel the world, play music I love, and watch people dance like maniacs.

18

A BIT MORE
DIGNIFIED?

PAYNO

I managed one day of Hask's week-long 40th birthday celebrations in Ibiza, flying out from Stansted at 7 a.m. and back to Luton at 2.30 a.m. the following morning – the perfect crime.

Hask had already done four days when I arrived and was in a pretty dire state, a shadow of the man I knew, although twice the man that finished the week. There were 20 of us in total, one of whom was yours truly, one of whom was Hask, 18 of whom were carbon copies of Hask. It was a great mass of biceps, aviator sunglasses, impossibly tight swimming trunks, testosterone and tattoos, and they had great fun toying with the lone beta male in their midst, like cats playing with a mouse.

Most of the chat was laced with dark humour, and real deep and meaningfuls were thin on the ground. Nobody was asking about other people's hopes and dreams, but if you turned up at Blue Marlin wearing the wrong shoes, that was a day's worth of material sorted.

His guests consisted of a few school mates, a few rugby mates, a couple of media characters, a couple of lads from the music world and other assorted reprobates Hask had met down the years. He's like a planet speeding through space, sucking like-minded people into his gravitational pull. His best friend Paul Doran-Jones was leading the charge as always, but it didn't really matter who was on the team sheet or what anybody else wanted to do. Hask was going to say a fond farewell to his 30s exactly the way he wanted, and he'd probably say that was one of the best weeks of his life. He's not a man to die wondering or have many regrets and I don't think turning 40 will change him in any way, shape or form. He's the Teflon Don, and he'll just keep rolling on and blasting through things.

While I'm sure Tins would have loved a few days in Ibiza, he tends to be more statesmanlike nowadays, as befits a member of the royal family. He's walked a fine line in the past but I think he now realises how high the stakes are. He keeps his Frank the Tank locked up, and we miss him.

In stark contrast to the hedonism of Ibiza, we recently did a photoshoot for a magazine called *The Rake*, which is a gentleman's quarterly that calls itself 'the modern voice of classic elegance'. It's run by a very nice gent called Tom Chamberlin, although I'm still confused as to why he saw fit to include us in his magazine.

While Tins got away with being dressed in a fairly stylish black dinner suit, and I was decked out in a slightly more adventurous velvet smoking jacket and slippers, Hask was photographed reclining on a chaise longue in a peacock silk dressing gown, with a cigar in his mouth and a Negroni by his side. I thought that was quite ironic given that he normally dresses like a ten-year-old, and some of his views on life are similarly child-like.

But maybe there's magic in that: when I'm in my dotage, spending most of my time sitting in front of a roaring fire with a blanket over my knees, Hask will probably still be dancing around a pool in Ibiza in his tiny swimming trunks. He'll definitely be more Wayne Lineker than Gary Lineker. Come to think of it, I think he's actually friends with Wayne.

HASK

For my DJing I'll highlight some clips on TikTok and kids will say stuff like, 'Someone come and collect your dad.' I'll think, *What the fuck are they talking about?*, because I don't feel old. Even when I played On The Beach (Carl Cox's big annual event) in Brighton a couple of years ago, it didn't bother me at all that most of the kids in the crowd were half my age.

DJing isn't really an age-specific game anyway, or so I think – Carl is in his sixties and he's just started a new residency at UNVRS in Ibiza. For most DJs now, it's about the music and whether you resonate with your audience. And while I'm very aware of the inexorable march of time – a daughter who's growing at an alarming rate, a face that's more creased than it once was, rugby careers that begin and end in the blink of an eye – my mind doesn't feel any older than 23. I'm more serious but I still have the same excitement for life, and I still have the capacity to act like an idiot. I'll sometimes think, *Am I supposed to be behaving differently now, just because I'm another year older?*

Alex speaks about wanting our brand to be more mature, classy and sophisticated, and that makes sense for him because he's always been older than his years. And while I get what he means about not wanting to be that dad making a tit of himself on the dancefloor, I reckon I will still be that dad on the dancefloor. I'll be that 70-year-old on testosterone replacement who's had a load of work done, lean as fuck in a tight polo shirt, Ferrari in the carpark, people tutting at me, and I won't give a shit.

Alex is a bit mixed up when it comes to this stuff anyway, because if we're doing a funny advert or anything like that, he takes it deadly seriously, and he always wants to win any challenge between the three of us. He can muck about like the best of us. My point being, I only usually get myself into trouble because, like him, I really care about whatever it is I'm doing, not because I'm some uncouth idiot. Well I am that as well, but at least I know I am.

I was DJing on a cruise ship during the 2023 World Cup, travelling from Marseille to Ibiza, and it ended up being a really bizarre evening. Some old bloke was standing at the front staring at me, as if he wanted to get my attention, forgetting that I couldn't just down tools and start having a chat with him. Someone else came up to me and shouted, 'My son's a really big fan, he used to go to school with so and so,' and I had to shout back, 'Mate, I can't chat now!' He got a bit arsey about it, because he didn't appreciate that I was in the middle of doing my job.

Another bloke kept staring at me, so I asked security to find out what he wanted. He came back and said, 'He wants to know if you're going to play any Eric Clapton.' I looked at this bloke and mouthed, 'No,' and he got in a huff and flounced out. I thought, *Did he really think I was going to segue from Route 94's 'My Love' to Eric Clapton's 'Wonderful Tonight'?*

Yet another bloke kept nodding and winking at me and his missus, and at first I thought he was suggesting a three-some, which wasn't really my vibe. I tried to ignore him, but eventually he wandered over holding this cuddly dragon and started trying to chat. I gave him the brush-off, before security informed me that he wanted me to know that his dragon had been at the 2015, 2019 and 2023 World Cups. I said to security, 'Mate, there's got to be more to that story, go and ask him again.' Alas, there was no more to that story.

The bloke smiled excitedly and gave me a thumbs-up, I responded with a small nod, and I could tell by his gesticulating and the frown on his missus's face that they were livid that I'd been unimpressed by his God-awful tale.

After I finished my set, some old drunk guy came up to me and started critiquing my performance. 'Can I give you some feedback on your set?' he said, to which I replied, 'No,' before he added, 'Look, you need to hear this, I used to play vinyl at my local working men's club.' I said, 'Listen, mate, I'm not interested in your opinion but thanks for sharing it and have a good night.' And walked off. I've definitely got blunter the older I've got, mainly because the alternative is getting sucked into an argument or being bored to death by some nause with a nonsensical story that basically ends up

235

with me having to listen to how amazing they are and how I could be better, which I really can't be bothered to do. I get that already spending time with Mike and Alex.

From there, I headed to the buffet in the VIP area, and while I was eating, the cuddly dragon bloke and his missus walked past. I tried not to make eye contact, but I could tell he'd clocked me, and while he was hovering, probably weighing up whether to give me a piece of his mind or not, I surreptitiously slipped out and hid by the railings on deck looking out over the inky black sea, as we had left port and were now steaming to Ibiza for a couple of days.

Unfortunately, this bloke followed me, grabbed me by the shoulder and whirled me around, brandishing his cuddly dragon, and said, 'You listen to me Haskell, I just think you're very rude. You need to understand that this dragon went to the World Cup in England in 2015, it went to the World Cup in Japan in 2019, and it's here now in France 2023.'

His body was trembling and his voice was cracking. He was steaming drunk as well, to make matters worse, but I still wasn't touched by his story. In fact, I grabbed this cuddly dragon out of his hand, and with the power of Zeus I launched it overboard and into the depths of the sea. If there was a world record for wanging a cuddly dragon, I reckon I smashed it. Then I said, 'Listen mate, if that fucking dragon makes it to Australia 2027, then that *is* a story.' While the bloke stared out into the dark white-capped waves in our huge boat's wake, tears were rolling down his face and he was going a deep purple and beginning to shake with anger. I legged it back to the VIP area, through a key-carded entrance and thick glass doors. He gave chase but I was safe behind the glass, which he was banging on, screaming, 'I will fucking get you for that, you wait, I will get you!' I just gave him the finger and walked off to bed.

I would like to say I felt some remorse, a modicum of shame or regret, but that would be bullshit. I slept like a baby who had thrown a dragon off a boat.

19

I THOUGHT I MIGHT PUNCH SOMEONE

TINS

I was first called up for England for the Centenary Test tour to Australia in 1999 (I dodged the 1998 'Tour of Hell' Down Under, when a young England team lost all seven games, including 76–0 to the Wallabies in Brisbane). I can't remember how I heard, but I may well have seen it on Ceefax, which was usually how things happened in those days.

I played in the tune-up against Queensland, which was when my friendship with Jason Leonard began. We only got one kit, so Jason gave me his jersey so I could swap it with my opposite number while hanging onto mine. It was such a great gesture, and I did the same with mine later on in my career.

I was also in the pre-1999 World Cup camp, but having trained like a lunatic, I got cut from the squad before the warm-up games. But when Jerry Guscott aggravated an injury during the pool game against Tonga, I was back in.

It was my 21st birthday and I was playing drinking golf with my Bath team-mate Nathan Thomas when I got the call from Clive Woodward, who sounded like a CIA operative. 'Are you able to talk?' said Clive, and I thought, *Well, yes, since I was about two.* 'Keep this completely to yourself, but Jerry's injured his groin. You need to come to Twickenham tomorrow. I need you in the squad for the rest of the tournament …' I half expected him to ask me to don a disguise.

Like the true professional I was, I celebrated my call-up by continuing to play drinking golf with Nathan. Well, it was my 21st birthday. That night, I locked myself out of Matt Perry's house, where I was living at the time, so had to phone a locksmith to let me in. He made a bit of a mess of Pezza's front door and I quickly packed and left, leaving the house wide open for anyone who fancied burgling it. When my head had cleared a bit, I asked a friend to get another locksmith to mend the door, before joining up with the England lads.

We beat Fiji but lost to South Africa in the quarter-final in Paris (when Jannie de Beer kicked five drop-goals), and I still had to wait until the following year's Six Nations before winning my first cap, against Ireland at Twickenham.

I knew I was in with a chance because quite a few players had retired, including the centre partnership of Jerry and Phil de Glanville, and I was playing well for Bath. But even though I'd been dreaming of playing for England for as long as I could remember, I didn't expect to get the call at 21.

A few of us youngsters made our international debuts that day – me, Benny Cohen, Steve Thompson, Iain Balshaw off the bench – and as first caps go, it was pretty sweet. Benny scored two tries, I scored one, and we demolished Ireland 50–18, our biggest ever win against them.

Mum and Dad were in the stands that day, carrying all the bad family nerves. I did get nervous, but it took the form of excitement, mixed with a bit of worry (playing for England back then was more about not making mistakes than expressing yourself). In contrast, Mum and Dad were always white as ghosts and looked like they were going to throw up when they watched me play for England.

There was a hierarchy in the England set-up, but Clive had brought in quite a few youngsters after the World Cup, and I was already friends with the Bath lads, so it wasn't an intimidating environment. Plus, we won my first four games, which was great for team bonding.

How we didn't win the Grand Slam that year I will never know, and that game against Scotland at Murrayfield will haunt me till my dying day. The Scots had been dismal all tournament, even losing to debutants Italy, but Duncan Hodge scored all their points in a 19–13 victory. I sometimes close my eyes and see the headline: SLAM DUNC.

We went out for a few beers after the game and got terrible abuse from Scotland fans. I was so angry that we'd lost that I honestly thought I might punch someone and eventually had to take myself back to the hotel.

Every rugby player must get used to losing, because it's an inevitable part of the sport. But it took me a long time, probably four or five years, to really learn how to let it go. I never learned to like losses, but I did learn to park and process them. As long as I could look at myself in the mirror and say, 'You gave everything you had,' that was good enough for me, as it was good enough for my dad when I was a kid.

I didn't speak to anyone about my attitude to losing, it just got to the point where I got bored of being miserable for days. That helps nothing and nobody, and far better to keep a clear head, review your performance and understand what you could do better.

Just like when I was a kid, I spent a lot of time analysing mistakes – *Did I put him in the wrong place in that tackle and miss the chance to get over the ball? Was the tackle too passive?* – but I quite enjoyed that anyway, although I wore my learning lightly. My England centre partner Will Greenwood would always talk about needing to learn his role in minute detail, but I did the same, while being more laid-back about it.

Looking back, the injury I suffered in 2001, which put me out of action for six months, probably helped change my perspective. I had microfractures in my femur, down by my knee, and the bone had gone kind of mushy. But the worst part about it was that nobody could tell me how long it would take to heal. I missed that year's Six Nations and the Lions tour to Australia, which I thought I had a decent chance of making. Brian O'Driscoll was definitely going to start the Tests, but I thought I might have partnered him had I been fit. It was very frustrating, but I think that time out made me a more philosophical person and more relaxed rugby player.

20

SMILE BECAUSE IT HAPPENED

PAYNO

While I never fulfilled my childhood dream of playing rugby for a living, I can empathise, at least a little bit, with retiring rugby players. My first ten years at Sky were a thrilling ride: the channel showed most of the best rugby available – the Premiership, the Heineken Cup, summer and autumn Internationals, Lions tours – and I was on board for all of it. It was like going on a stag do every week, with some broadcasting thrown in.

I once flew to Belfast to cover an Ulster Heineken Cup game at a packed Ravenhill on the Thursday, drove to Dublin for Leinster v Agen for the Friday evening (when the great Rupeni Caucaunibuca gave Brian O'Driscoll the run-around), got a private jet to Geneva, where Munster were playing Bourgoin, on the Friday evening, before heading up to Chamonix for a few days' skiing with some workmates. It was five days of great European cities, thronging pubs and bars, rock star rugby players, incredible games, private jets, and snow sport, and we did much the same the following week.

Back then, working for Sky Sports had a certain glamour, while also being wonderfully chaotic. I'd argue that it was probably as much fun as you could possibly have while calling it work and many of my colleagues became great friends. We played corridor cricket for hours, had a Sky rugby team, frequented Windsor Racecourse on Mondays off, went to each other's birthday parties and weddings.

I'll never forget the constant games of spoof, in the office and TV trucks, with the loser having to buy 20 cups of coffee for the group, but it was also larger-than-life TV executives backing creative people and saying, 'Whatever you want to do, go and do it.'

Although it was great fun, I reached a point when I was working 42 weekends a year which was hard on my wife. She attended untold weddings and birthday parties without me and had many years of looking after our young children at weekends.

Having said that, the flip side is that I was lucky enough to attend more of my kids' ballets recitals, swimming lessons and school concerts than most dads because I was around a lot during the week. And while I made sacrifices, and probably missed out on some great occasions, I was having unbelievable experiences working for Sky instead, so I wouldn't have changed a thing. I am very, very lucky to have had the best seat on so many occasions.

One of my favourite memories is England v New Zealand in 2012. England had been pretty ordinary so far that autumn, losing to Australia and South Africa, but when I arrived at Twickenham that day, I distinctly remember there was this feeling they had a puncher's chance to do something special. It was just one of those days when English defiance was at its best – written off, and ready to do something about it.

Having breakfast in the food truck in the TV compound with Miles Harrison and Stuart Barnes, we were chatting about the game and I can still remember the sense that 'this might be on' rather than 'they've got no chance'. England fans hadn't experienced many really special days since the 2003 World Cup final, but that day might be one that they remember for many years to come.

That was probably the biggest game I'd done as a presenter at the time, so I felt a big weight of pressure and expectation. But I also felt very privileged to be part of the storytelling team for such a big occasion. The All Blacks were reigning world champions, were looking to go unbeaten that year, and had an unbelievable team. England, meanwhile, were still trying to find their feet after their average showing at the 2011 World Cup, and people wondered if head coach Stuart Lancaster was the right man for the job. But England had some pretty good players, including a certain J. Haskell, and every now and again the beast can wake from its slumber and put its fangs to good use.

As it turned out, England were magnificent that day, beating New Zealand – McCaw, Carter et al. – 38–21, their biggest ever win against them. But while it was a real team effort, there was no doubt about the man of the match: Manu Tuilagi, who announced himself as one of the most devastating attacking forces in world rugby and somehow managed to outshine the All Blacks' vaunted centre partnership of Ma'a Nonu and Conrad Smith.

As wonderful as it was to bear witness to such a great performance by England, afterwards was probably even more special. If you'd told me when I was a kid, 'One day, you'll be in a television studio at Twickenham, discussing a famous England victory over the All Blacks with Sir Clive Woodward, Jonny Wilkinson and Will Greenwood,' I'd have told you to stop being so daft. It was one of those pinch-me moments, the cherry on top of a day that I'll never forget.

Nothing lasts forever, good or bad, and the beginning of the end of Sky Sport's glory years was when Vic Wakeling and the hierarchy of Premiership Rugby failed to see eye to eye on a new deal. Premiership Rugby completely disappeared from Sky's schedules in 2013, after which they lost the rights to European rugby in 2017 and the Pro12 (now the United Rugby Championship) in 2018. It was a pretty depressing experience to go through: every six months another set of broadcasting rights was lost and it became apparent that Sky just weren't prepared to fight for rugby union anymore. I don't remember being particularly worried about my future at Sky – although I clearly should have been – but I thought there were still plenty of options for me there. However, the whole process meant I wasn't enjoying working there as much as I once had.

For example, the kids would get home from school at 4 p.m. on a Friday, really excited about the weekend, and I'd have to drive to Luton Airport at 4.30 for a Saturday game of no real importance in Glasgow or Galway. We'd have a five-minute build-up, because kick-off would be straight off the back of a football match, five minutes' chat at half-time and a five-minute build-down, and hardly anyone was watching anyway.

Some of that was simply down to changing viewing habits: when I was young, I'd watch all the build-up and all the build-down, but there were only three Sky Sports channels back then. Now, the options are never-ending: TNT, Premier, Eurosport and others, so people tend to tune in when the game kicks off and tune out as soon as the final whistle goes, with only rugby afficionados doing the real deep dive. Regardless, what had once seemed like the most exciting job in the world now seemed like a bit of a grind. I'd fallen out of love with it, although a decent pay cheque will blind you to that truth.

Not only was Sky losing chunks of its once spectacular rugby portfolio, it was also about to be bought out by mass media conglomerate Comcast, so it began to strip assets – including people. There were rounds and rounds of redundancies, but I still didn't see the writing on the wall.

We still had Super Rugby, the Rugby Championship and a chunk of England games, Championship rugby and summer tours. I was lead presenter, and I thought my job was to keep the show on the road and everyone jollying along. I also thought that if we lost rugby altogether, I'd carry on working for Sky, even if it meant moving to a different sport. Maybe *FishOMania* would have me back?

Barney Francis had taken over from Vic Wakeling as managing director in 2009, and it was proving very difficult to nail him down as to what my contract situation was. We had a couple of fleeting conversations but nothing concrete. The situation dragged and dragged until there were only five months before my contract was due to run out. I managed to secure a meeting with his deputy and the executive producer, and I rather blindly thought that I'd walk into his office, he'd slide a new three-year contract across the desk, I'd shake his hand and say thank you, and off I'd go.

The day before my meeting, I messaged a producer I was close to, asking how he'd got on in a similar meeting he'd had that morning. He didn't reply until midnight, which I immediately thought was odd and was the response of a man who didn't really want to talk. I had a really nagging feeling, and my wife said, 'Why don't you go in and see him tomorrow ahead of your meeting?'

So I went in early to catch him, and he was really evasive, and when I finally said to him, 'Do I need to be worried about this?', he paused and then replied, 'It's not the meeting you think it is. You need to be prepared.'

Adrenaline was coursing through my veins when I walked in for my discussion. I had no idea what was coming, but at least I wouldn't be blindsided and I knew I'd have to fight to get as much out of it as I could. Barney's deputy didn't turn up on time, so after 20 minutes or so of waiting, I asked my executive producer what was going on. 'Look,' he said, 'I'm really sorry, but you've got five months and you're out. We just don't have enough rugby anymore.'

Even though I knew it wasn't going to be a great meeting, I hadn't expected it to be that brutal. I couldn't believe that having built me into a relatively useful commodity, they were just going to cut me loose. I was 37, had a wife, two young kids, a mortgage, a car, and it all flashed before my eyes. Then I regained some composure. Sky was still showing England games, so I asked who was going to present them when I was gone. He said they were looking at options, and I suggested that I could do it on a pay-as-I-play basis. 'That's actually quite a good idea,' he replied. 'Why don't you go home and write me a proposal.'

In the proposal, I explained that as the home of England rugby, Sky should really have an English person presenting the coverage, and that I'd like to do the four autumn Internationals, three summer Test matches, plus any other bits and bobs. They thought that was fair enough and ended up paying me a day rate that was way more than I was expecting, stopped me from going into financial freefall and kept me relevant in the game. But I went from 42 weekends a year to seven. After 15 years I was no longer a part of Sky, and I found myself totally skittled.

In quick succession, the great and good of what had been a fine rugby department departed, including my old studio pals Stuart Barnes and Dewi Morris, who had been by my side on many a great rugby occasion. Graham Simmons took redundancy, commentators Miles Harrison and Mark Robson moved on. Fellow presenter James Gemmell headed back to New Zealand. It was a very sad end to what had been a hell of a journey. A lot of people were very angry, and the jungle drums didn't stop beating for months.

We'd been a very tight bunch, had formed some great friendships and really looked after each other for many years, and now we were being scattered to the winds. And it wasn't just about loss of earnings for most people, it was about loss of identity. I'd walk into a room and people would want to talk to me about the fact I worked for Sky Sports, and now I had to tell people I didn't do that anymore. I was terrified, just as a rugby player must be terrified when he wakes up one Monday morning and remembers that he's no longer wanted by his club or his sport.

When I finally sloped out of Sky HQ for the final time, I couldn't help but feel it was a very different place to the one I'd walked into in 2001. It had made the well-trodden move from challenger to establishment, the accountants ran the show, not the creatives and it had become a corporate beast.

Whereas you used to be able to sense the creative buzz throughout its long corridors and packed offices – and hear those riotous games of spoof – now it's a slick machine that just rolls on. It has been brilliant to dip the toe back in on occasion, and catching up with a number of familiar faces while covering the Lions tour to Australia was a treat. There are a lot of good people within the walls who have created some incredible sports TV over the years.

I always thought Sky asked for a lot of loyalty from those who worked there, which leads to a strong sense of belonging. Understandably, a few of those who left at the same time were very bruised by their departure. I remember telling myself I wasn't going to let my exit eat me up. For the most part, my attitude has been don't cry because it's over, smile because it happened.

As much as I felt like everything I'd worked for had been snatched from me, just when I was getting comfortable, and as much as I felt like I'd lost my identity, I had to keep saying to myself, *Don't waste time griping about this. You've got to get going again.*

The worst moment in my broadcasting career eventually led to the best thing in my broadcasting career, and my greatest satisfaction is leaving mainstream media and building something of my own (with Hask and Tins, of course), and something that has proved to be more fun and more rewarding.

I've been in a few pits of despair during my time with *The Good, The Bad & The Rugby*, not least when we ended up mired in that court case, which we spoke about at length in the first book. But it's all part of the story, and I wouldn't change a thing about my journey. I have been so very, very lucky to end up in the places I have. And I know there's more to come.

21

INJECT IT AND STRAP IT

TINS

I'm writing this just after the first Test between the Lions and Australia in July 2025, and the Wallabies have been criticised for not looking like they cared enough about losing. It's a common criticism of modern players but it's just not true.

Some fans seem to think they care more than players but losing hurts players more than any fan can possibly understand. Just because they're chatting with the opposition or smiling or holding their baby doesn't mean they don't care, they're just trying to deal with defeat in a way that's healthy for them.

I got heaps of criticism pretty much from my first England appearance, mainly because you can't be everyone's cup of tea. That was a massive learning curve for me – you have to figure out whose criticism matters! Coaches, team-mates, family and friends, if they are happy with everything you are doing then you are probably on the right track. You also need to be your own harshest critic;

if you can do that then you should be able to deal with everyone else.

Stuart Barnes on Sky's *The Rugby Club* was the guy who doubted me the most and for a long time I really disliked him. The best example of this was before Bath played Saracens at their place in January 2001. I had hurt my hand and had been advised not to play the game, then on Thursday night I was watching *The Rugby Club* and they were looking at players who should be playing for England in the Six Nations. Stuart said I wasn't good enough to play and that really pissed me off as I felt I was playing well at the time. I went straight to the physios' room and told him I had to play – 'Inject it and strap it, I'm starting.' I was up against Tim Horan that day, who I regarded as one of the best in the game. I managed to run through him to score one (unfortunately knocking him out), before getting over again later in the game. It was one of those games where everything went my way. We ended up winning 31–11 and I gave it to Stuart in my post-match interview. In hindsight, I should have thanked him because had he not said what he did, I wouldn't have played at all.

It was criticism that made me keep getting off the floor when I had almost nothing left, but there was a time in 2005–06 when the criticism became too much. Andy Robinson had replaced Clive Woodward as England head coach in 2004 and everything that went wrong during his time in charge seemed to be blamed on the centres. It didn't matter if it was me and Jamie Noon, Noony and Mat Tait (even though they'd played together God knows how many times for Newcastle) or Noony and Olly Barkley, we were always seen as the problem. I even got flak after winning man of the match against Italy.

I kept reading articles about how Will Greenwood could never be replaced, but nobody ever offered a solution, and when Robbo dropped me for the final Six Nations game in 2006, I was relieved, because it meant I wasn't going to be abused for a week. I can laugh about it now, but it wasn't funny at the time. All I could do was go out, give it my all, and hope to prove people wrong.

Public criticism is part and parcel of sport at the highest level, but the problem is with how it's done in England. Fast-forward to the summer of 2025. A lot of people thought that Tom Curry shouldn't start the first Test between the Lions and Australia, which is fine, because maybe other flankers had played better than him up until then (or that was people's perception). The issue was people who had no real right to comment claiming he wasn't good enough, which was obviously nonsense because he ended up being the best player on the park and scoring a try. Anyone who plays international rugby is an elite performer, but people will have opinions on who they prefer and want to voice this. The players just have to listen to it – they have very little control of it and no way of avoiding it.

In America, people are more inclined to praise athletes. Even if they're off form, journalists and broadcasters will make sure to say how good they are, whereas in England, they often lack that balance. Owen Farrell is a perfect example. All he's ever done is give his best for England, but perhaps because he comes across quite dour, he's become a pantomime villain for some.

Never mind that he's won over a hundred international caps, and been on four Lions tours, and that everyone he's played with describes him as the ultimate competitor, people still boo him. I'm sure Owen was like me for most of his career, someone who used the criticism as fuel, but I'm not surprised he went to France for a break, because it does eat away at you, however tough you are.

I enjoy chatting to Stuart Barnes now, and while I still disagree with some of his views on rugby, I understand that as a columnist in a national newspaper, it's his job to fire people up. He's argumentative, and like all good debaters, he's got no qualms about changing his argument to fit a certain narrative. And he understands that being nice doesn't sell, as they say in the newspaper world.

Having said that, I sense the overall mood changing. Media criticism isn't as harsh as it used to be, and journalists are more likely to accept that form can ebb and flow, and good players don't suddenly become terrible overnight.

22

GEECH'S FUNNY TURN

PAYNO

Lions tours have always meant the most to me, and Sir Ian McGeechan is the godfather of all things Lions, having toured with them twice as a player and five times as a coach, with much success. As you can imagine, he's the most extraordinary man to be around whenever they're in action.

Every sport nowadays is searching for a younger audience, but perhaps the most important thing about the Lions as an institution is its history, and Geech is Lions history personified. He played all four Tests in 1974, when the Lions put the Springboks to the sword, and coached the Lions to series victories in 1989 and 1997. And while he didn't match that success on subsequent tours, he was involved with the Lions as late as South Africa 2009.

I was lucky enough to work with Sir Ian in 2013, 2017 and 2021, and I did so again in 2025, even though he'd recently been diagnosed with prostate cancer. As you can imagine, I've got lots of great memories alongside Geech – but one quite scary one.

Back in 2017, the Lions had been blown off the park by New Zealand in the first Test in Auckland, which made a bit of a mockery of all the pre-tour hype. I'll never forget walking down to Wellington's Westpac Stadium, as it was then, on the morning of the second Test and having a very gloomy chat with Sky commentator Miles Harrison. It was cold, it was grey, it was raining, and we were shuffling along like a couple of kids on our way to detention. Neither of us could see how the Lions could possibly win. The All Blacks, we thought, were simply in a different league, and would surely seal the series.

We all gathered for a bit of food, before I headed up to the studio at about four o'clock, to get ready for a six o'clock start. When I first plugged my earpiece into the audio, there was the usual chatter, before things suddenly went very quiet. I was sitting there, watching the clock and thinking, *We've only got 60 minutes until we're on air, what's going on?*, until someone finally informed me that Geech had been taken ill and rushed to hospital. In true Geech fashion, he'd been very apologetic as they helped him into the ambulance.

Our executive producer had gone with him, which was obviously the right thing to do, but he was meant to be running our show. The minutes ticked by, and with half an hour until we were due on air, everyone was in limbo with no news, nor any idea what was going on. A plan was being formulated that we were going to scrap the one-hour build-up, fill it with highlights and I would come on air a minute before the teams ran out, explain the situation and throw to Miles and Stuart in commentary. There was a great deal of concern for Sir Ian. We all rather sat on our hands and twiddled our thumbs, waiting.

However, ten minutes before the scheduled on-air time, our executive producer called in to say that Geech was feeling much better – he'd had a sugary drink, loosened his tie, made himself comfortable in his hospital bed, and that he'd really like the show to go on as planned. What a guy, and obviously – what a relief.

Unfortunately though, we now had about seven minutes to get ourselves ready for the build-up to the biggest broadcast I'd ever been involved in, a potentially deciding Test between the Lions and New Zealand. I just had to take a deep breath and dive into it. We came on air, I explained Geech's absence, said that he'd made contact, was doing better and would be watching from his hospital bed. I then blagged the rest of it.

The Lions were dreadful for most of the game and trailed 18–9 with 20 minutes to go, despite Sonny Bill Williams getting a red card midway through the first half. It seemed for all the world as though the Lions were going to blow the most golden of opportunities. But Taulupe Faletau scored to give the tourists hope, Conor Murray went over ten minutes later to level the scores at 21–21, before Owen Farrell's late penalty won it for the Lions.

A day that had started so gloomily, before taking a terrifying turn, had blossomed into a euphoric broadcast. That was the Lions in a nutshell: events coming at us from all angles, while we just tried to hold on, hoping the story ended up in the right place.

The build-down after the game was almost like a celebration (although possibly not for Sean Fitzpatrick) and our studio was swamped by Lions fans in full voice and full of beer. But as we tried to pick through the glory and the moment, there was this almighty scuffle among the supporters behind us. Live on air, I turned around to see my brother, who had been drinking all day, trying to climb through a window into the studio to say hello. The kerfuffle was him being dragged away and ejected from the stadium by three Maori security guards. I can picture it now: 'Not the face! I'm Alex Payne's brother!' 'Who the hell is Alex Payne, bro?'

So one of the proudest moments of my broadcasting career collided with one of my brother's most disappointing public performances, leaving our mother with rather contrasting emotions. To finish off an extraordinary day, it was actually his birthday, and for many reasons there was a lot to celebrate. As I said, the Lions comes at you from everywhere.

It turned out that Geech had just had a funny turn – something he'd eaten, not enough water, who knows – and he wanted minimum fuss when he rejoined us for the third Test the following week. His recent diagnosis in 2025 was rather more serious, but it was great to hear he had been given the all-clear on the eve of this year's Lions tour. After four Lions tours together in the studio, he sent a really kind message after this year's tour was done and dusted, one of those I'll keep in the scrapbook.

The Lions tour of 2025 certainly had them back where they should be – full stadiums, huge travelling support, last-gasp drama. It was all in stark contrast to South Africa in 2021, which wasn't a great experience. It was in the middle of the Covid pandemic, there were no fans and the rugby was pretty average. Having said that, I did enjoy the uncertainty at times. We came on air before one game, between the Lions and the Sharks in Durban, not knowing if it would go ahead or not. We had no idea which Lions players had travelled, or even if they had enough players to form a squad. I actually found myself thinking back to the early days on Sky Sports News and remembering the fear of breaking news. Now the fun bit is trying to work out what's going on in real time with an audience ready and waiting. Telling a story without knowing where you're trying to get to is a lot of fun.

At the time of writing, I'm just back from my seventh Lions tour, and the third time I've been to Australia. While down there, I couldn't help but compare them all – the raw excitement of being the tea boy in 2001, the enormous pressure of presenting my first tour in 2013, and the fun and enjoyment of doing it in 2025. Twenty-four years of following the Lions as well as over 20,000 hours of live broadcasting with Sky and covering over 500 Test matches. If you'd told the ten-year-old watching *Bill's Best Bits* that's what I'd be able to write on my CV, I reckon I'd have taken it.

Without going all Steve Redgrave and 'never again', I think it is likely to be the last time I work for Sky. It just feels like leaving it in Australia, where for me it all began, has a nice synergy to it. And if it is to be the case, then my final game was a Lions Test in Sydney. In pouring, biblical rain.

We knew it was going to be wet, and our production team had sent a message in the Sky WhatsApp group telling everyone to come prepared as we were broadcasting pitchside throughout the game. So on the morning of the third Test I headed into Sydney, found an outdoor shop and bought myself some waterproofs and boots. For a total of $50.

I'll admit they weren't catwalk material, but when I put them on at the stadium as we prepared to go on air, I was torn to shreds by Warren Gatland, John Barclay, Dan Biggar and Will Greenwood. The rain had not yet arrived, and the ridicule began to make me panic. But having taken ten minutes to put all the clobber on, I didn't have time to undo it all – I was pot committed, I just had to park my dignity in these nylon trousers and hope that the heavens would open to justify my gamble.

Which they did. Jesus, did they. I have never, ever seen anything like it. And as we battled away pitchside – amid notes washed away, umbrellas blown inside out, electrics fusing, lightning strikes – my warm sense of smug began to grow. Our build-up was 90 minutes long, throughout which I just smiled. Those alongside, in their suits and chinos and white trainers, lost their sense of humour. When we eventually took our seats pitchside for the game to begin, Warren Gatland – a three-time Lions head coach – had water running down his back and out through his trouser leg. He was essentially a drain pipe.

As we huddled under a single umbrella, he leant over and told me that he thought his pants had dissolved, and his trousers were going too. I looked at his shoes, and they were like pulped cardboard boxes.

'I'm sorry to hear that, Warren,' I replied, as I brushed a single water molecule off my nylon trousers.

'You bastard,' he replied.

As the final chapter closed on what has been a wonderful, wonderful ride, I'm tempted to amend the old saying – for players, coaches or presenters: 'One day you're the cock of the walk, the next you're sitting in mulched shoes.'

23

I'VE NO IDEA WHO
THIS BLOKE IS

PAYNO

The month the three of us spent together in Japan for the 2019 World Cup is difficult to top, and I'm not sure we ever will.

We saw some unbelievable games, including England thumping Australia and England outplaying the All Blacks in the semi-finals. South Africa were very average in beating Wales in their semi-final, and I'll never forget standing under the posts 20 minutes before the final kicked off and thinking, *I cannot see any way that England lose this game …*

Wow, hindsight is a wonderful thing.

As well as being out there with the podcast, I was also hosting the in-stadium entertainment on match days. Before the England v New Zealand game, we finished our pitchside chat with a few minutes to go until kick-off and were taken in through a door and along a corridor to get up to our seats. I've no idea how it happened, but I somehow got separated from the others and ended up going through a service door into the back of the England changing room. I must have taken a wrong turn and gone through a security or tradesman's entrance, but I couldn't get out the same way, and as I was working out how to escape, the England team started filing in. They'd finished their warm-up, and this was their final moment together before running out for the anthems in a World Cup semi-final. I was stuck in rugby's holiest of holies at the worst possible time.

I tried to hide behind a door, but I was that bloke off the telly, wearing a suit and holding a microphone and clipboard, so couldn't have looked more conspicuous if I'd tried. A few of the players and coaches were like, 'What the fuck are you doing in here?' I slid towards the main exit, back to the wall, and couldn't help thinking of that scene in *Four Weddings and a Funeral*, where Hugh Grant gets caught in a bedroom with the newly wed couple going hammer and tongs, and he suddenly jumps up with a pencil in his hand and says, 'Found it!' As someone who's worked pretty hard over the years to respect the boundaries between players and the media, and has always tried quite hard to keep out of the way, I'm not sure I've ever found myself in quite such a wrong place at the wrong time. Had England lost that game, I might have been part of the inquest. As it was, it was forgotten about in the euphoria of reaching the final.

And those boundaries are real. Most sportspeople are accommodating when it comes to interviews and the like, but on game day be very careful if you enter the Lions' den. I'll never forget covering a 2019 World Cup warm-up game between England and Wales in Cardiff. I was pitchside with Will Greenwood and Maggie Alphonsi, and we ended up broadcasting from exactly where England wanted to do their line-out practice. I had a director saying, 'All of you step back, I want you to be as close to the action as possible,' and Steve Borthwick saying, 'Get off my fucking pitch! You're interrupting our warm-up! How much longer are you gonna be?'

No two ways about it, Steve is a phenomenal coach, but step into his kingdom on match day, particularly as a member of the media, and being in his vicinity is like entering his house uninvited at midnight. And while I could understand his reaction, there are two sides to a situation like that. He's protecting his patch because he's trying to prepare his team for a game and he feels intruded on, but we're trying to tell the story as well as possible so that people watching at home feel like they're part of it.

Alongside the podcast and lots of corporate activity, I was hosting the in-stadium experience in Japan. I was on the mic, linking in and out of highlights and interviews, with a lovely Japanese co-host, and we were in charge of building the atmosphere for 85,000 people in the stadium. One of my jobs in the final was getting the crowd to decide if they wanted to hear 'Sweet Caroline' or 'Take Me Home, Country Roads', which was mildly cruise-ship entertainer but good fun.

The crowd had the choice, and I reckon 80,000 people cheered for Neil Diamond. But because my dad loves a bit of John Denver, and I knew he'd be watching at home, I said, 'OK everyone! You've voted to go with 'Take Me Home, Country Roads'!' 80,000 people booed, 5,000 people sang along, of which I was the loudest. But it had to be done.

You wouldn't have thought it watching me that day, but I've never really been very interested in the limelight, and I've never been particularly keen to share my story. It has always been about the game – I wouldn't be doing this in any other field. But I was tempted into doing some corporate gigs in the early part of my career, including commentating on plastic ducks floating down the Thames one sunny afternoon at Hampton Court, for which I was paid the princely sum of £500. I remember thinking, 'This is absolutely incredible. I'm literally being paid to commentate on a duck race.'

When the same agency that got me the duck gig very kindly booked me to do an end-of-season dinner at Cheltenham Rugby Club, I couldn't believe my luck. I was still paying off my student debt, so another £500 for not much work felt almost like a lottery win. But the closer it got to the dinner, the more I started to think, *I don't actually know what I'm doing. And I've only been on the telly five minutes. I'm not actually sure this is a very good idea.*

I only got the gig because former England lock Martin Bayfield – the best in the business – pulled out, so I phoned him and asked how I should play it. Martin, who had been doing these kinds of gigs for years, advised me to keep it short – between 10 to 15 minutes – and crack a couple of gags. 'You'll be in and out in no time,' he assured me. I still wasn't entirely convinced, I'm not sure he was either, but there was no backing out.

I wrote my speech the day before and arrived in Cheltenham in plenty of time, but I knew I was in a whole world of trouble as soon as I arrived at the venue. Nobody had any idea who I was or why I was there, and I got the impression that most people had turned up expecting to see Martin Bayfield. It reminded me of that episode of *Alan Partridge* when he announces that Sue Cook has pulled out of an event and disappointed audience members head for the exit. But that was just the start of my humiliation.

The rugby club's chair introduced me with the words, 'I've no idea who this bloke is, or what he does, but would you please welcome Alex Payne from Sky Sports …' Things went rapidly downhill from there. I tried to crack a couple of gags, as Martin had suggested, but nobody laughed. After about three minutes, an entire table got up and filed out of the marquee, before returning five minutes later, all stark bollock naked. Obviously, everyone found that hilarious, which made my own attempts at humour seem even more feeble.

It was an absolute car crash, and I was so embarrassed that I stopped speaking and sat down after a couple of minutes. Total surrender. If I remember rightly, the chairman stood up and said, 'I'm not sure what that was, but please show your appreciation.' There was barely a ripple, after which I slunk out the back, jumped into my car and got the hell out of there. I'm sure the desolate screech of my tyres could be heard throughout the West Country.

That was a truly awful experience, I still wince when I think about it, and I still have the mental scars, but it taught me a crucial lesson, namely that you should stay in your lane and stick to what you're good at. You're stepping into the lion's den doing rugby club dinners. It's *their* night, they all want to get absolutely pie-eyed, and you've got to be very, very good to step into that environment, own it for 20 minutes and escape with your dignity intact. And it simply wasn't my thing.

I've always been much more interested in other people's stories and love bringing the best out of the people around me. One of the things I find most rewarding about the pod is when we have someone on and listeners say, 'I used to think he was a dick, but I actually really like him.' And I'm comfortable cruising along in my lane, trying to remain on track and getting people to buy into what we're trying to do, while leaving the comedy routines to people like Hask.

I have never wanted to be the story, but sometimes you end up getting dragged into it. A couple of years ago, I presented a game between the Barbarians and a World XV on Channel 5, alongside former England prop David Flatman and former England women's international Shaunagh Brown. At one point I linked to an interview with World XV coach Steve Hansen, and when they came back to me, I said, 'Well, you can see why he was a policeman', because he'd been very tight-lipped. But as soon as I said it, Shaunagh jumped in with, 'I think you mean police officer ...'

I said 'Yep, beg your pardon,' and moved on. Everyone's entitled to their opinion and I'm not someone who's looking for an argument. I knew that had I even hesitated or raised an eyebrow – let alone said, 'Policeman, police officer, whatever' – I've left my lane, and it becomes a storm in a teacup. But of course social media lit up – for Shaunagh, for me for not pushing back, for Channel 5 for being woke. It was utterly exhausting, and a total waste of everyone's time.

People are entitled to have their own viewpoint, and I'm happy to accept their viewpoint and crack on. I have a very simple perspective on life: does a disagreement add to my day? Does it make me happier? To which the answer is almost always no. The world is a very angry place at the moment, but I'm trying very hard to make my ride as smooth as possible. If the sun is shining and my family are well, I'm in a good place.

Of course, Hask takes a very different view, and I'm not sure how he'd react if someone picked him up on 'problematic' language live on air. I suspect what followed would resemble an Alan Partridge skit, which is maybe why television companies don't phone him anymore.

24

NOT A REBEL
LEAGUE

TINS

Rugby is an unbelievable game – tough, skilful and built on values – but it hasn't moved with the times. If it doesn't evolve, it risks becoming yesterday's sport. This is precisely why I'm so excited by R360 – it's about unlocking rugby's massive international potential, not reinventing it.

R360 is a huge global project. And it's bloody exciting. I'm pretty full-time on it now, and we're not launching until late 2026! I can't wait to see it come to life. For me it's exactly the shot in the arm that rugby needs. Cricket, tennis, golf, F1 and even darts are all transforming by tapping into younger generations of fans to unlock greater commercial opportunities for the players. Now it's rugby's turn.

R360 is designed to be the new apex of club rugby. In an F1-style competition, we'll be taking the best players in the world around the globe. Kicking off in October 2026, it will have a grand-prix-style first season with six events, then in 2027 – because of the World Cup and Women's Lions – we'll host 12 events before moving to the full schedule of

16 events in 2028. Each event will be hosted over three days in cities such as Barcelona, Miami, Hong Kong and London, to name but a few.

There will be a draft approach that takes its lead from how NFL creates theatre, and we'll be making the events themselves a beautiful combination of entertainment and sport. Season one will commence with six men's and four women's franchise teams, growing to ten men's teams by 2028. The feedback from players, coaches and fans has been incredibly positive – it's clear the motivation is there.

Rugby is being left behind. Club rugby has long been in the headlines for all the wrong financial reasons. Unlike most professional sports, rugby relies heavily on the international game to keep the club game afloat – and the cracks are showing. In recent years we've seen proud names like Wasps, Worcester and London Irish disappear in England, the Melbourne Rebels fold in Australia, multiple MLR franchises in the US collapse, and teams in Japan step away from professionalism.

The truth is that the club game is drastically under-commercialised. Too often, the model for growth has been stuck in the past: play more matches, raise ticket prices and sell more pints. That's not a sustainable strategy in today's sports and entertainment landscape. Compare that with football, where global club competitions like the Champions League generate billions in broadcast rights, or the IPL in cricket, which created a brand-new product and transformed player salaries and fan engagement almost overnight. The NBA and NFL thrive because their leagues are designed as entertainment products first and foremost, built around scarcity, spectacle and storytelling.

Rugby hasn't unlocked that formula. Right now, there are 96 professional rugby clubs worldwide – yet only a few of them make a profit, and almost none make money from rugby alone. Most unions are either in debt or only just climbing out of it, while still carrying the responsibility for every part of the game in their countries, from grassroots to international. It's a system that anyone can see simply doesn't add up, and it's holding rugby back.

The Men's Rugby World Cup is consistently one of the biggest global sporting events, with up to 800 million people engaging with it. In the UK, England's World Cup semi-final against South Africa in 2023 was watched by 8.7 million people. There's clearly a massive interest in the top end of the game, but there are only 24 million club fans worldwide, so what happens to the other 776 million fans who are engaging with the World Cup? The circa 200 million fans that connect with international rugby every year? That's where R360 comes in. We feel there's a gap in the market for a truly global league, with the best players in the world going up against each other, for people who want to see it but don't normally get the chance to.

One of the most exciting opportunities is the women's game. The recent World Cup has shown the appetite – sold-out stadiums, record-breaking viewing figures and the emergence of players who are genuine global stars in their own right. Yet between those peaks, there simply aren't enough regular moments for fans to connect with the women's game. R360 can change that.

By putting men and women side by side – sharing the same platform, broadcast visibility, fan experience and storytelling – we can accelerate growth like never before. This is about creating rivalries that capture imaginations, new heroes for kids to look up to and year-round opportunities for players to shine.

And it's not just about visibility. It's about professionalising conditions properly: equal access to the best coaches, medical support, commercial opportunities and global exposure. That's how you go from one-off spikes of interest to sustained fandom. If rugby gets this right, women's rugby can be one of the fastest-growing sports in the world. When it comes to the rapidly growing women's game, we again see the international stage proving the catalyst for engaging new fans – with this year's record-breaking Women's Rugby World Cup attendance and TV/online viewership. And of course, big shout out to Ilona Maher for showing how it's done when it comes to the social-content play.

As for the players themselves, the NFL understands that scarcity can be a good thing, which is why teams only play 17 regular season games. In contrast, every time rugby wants to make more money, historically it adds more games, and the international players then get punished most for being at the top of their game. And while international players' workloads are increasing far beyond what they should, salaries are generally stalling or decreasing because of salary caps, reducing squad sizes. If you look at the academy system, we're seeing more and more burgeoning talents having their potential careers cut short due to the financial constraints, with players simply cut from the squad with nowhere to go (other than the Championship – which, as we know, has its own challenges as a professional league offering). Players don't often let the side down, and they know their worth, and R360 aims to bring $200m of new money into the game – surely that's a good thing.

R360 is definitely not a 'rebel league'. We're focused on one thing, and one thing only – to benefit rugby. I'm confident R360 will lift the game up for everyone in the years to come. And we'll do it by taking learnings from what's gone before us across the worlds of sport and entertainment, and translating it to work for rugby. It is a new format. That's undoubted and we are unapologetic about it. We have the data and the insight to back up decisions we're making, and the expertise around us to deliver brilliantly. We will hold onto the traditions that make rugby so special, but not shy away from the combat sport it is. It's brutal at times, but also beautiful. We want this to be celebrated like never before.

People will call it a threat. But if doing nothing is the alternative, the real threat is rugby slowly withering on the vine. Comparisons have been made to Kerry Packer's World Series Cricket, which attracted some of the world's greatest cricketers in the 1970s and changed the face of the sport forever. But it's often forgotten that Packer tried to do something similar with rugby when the game went pro in 1995. About 400 players signed provisional contracts for Packer's World Rugby Corporation, including most of the New Zealand, Australia and South Africa squads. But while England's top players were weighing up whether to sign or not, the South African players, who had been told by their union that they'd never play for the Springboks again if they jumped ship, pulled out.

Looking at the mess rugby is in now, I think not going with Packer's plan could have been an error. I'm not blaming anyone in particular, but unions trying to do their best for the amateur and pro games just hasn't worked, and clubs that were amateur entities for decades have never been able to decipher what the game should look like in the professional age. Separating the professional club game from the unions and letting it thrive in its own space, while allowing the international game to continue feels the right step forward.

Sport is full of these moments where someone dares to challenge the traditional model – and history usually shows they were right. At the end of the day, we believe rugby can thrive at the cutting edge of sports entertainment if the right structures and systems are in place. By elevating everything across fan, player and media experience, R360 will boost broad youth appeal, amplify global cultural relevance and deliver a brilliant new product to rugby fans everywhere.

The broadcast strategy is critical to our approach – and we're excited to have a new free-to-air model in place that will reduce barriers for the younger fans to see their stars on screens. But the truth is that how younger generations (our future for the sport) consume sport has changed. This is why we're working with leading gaming and youth-content teams to help take the game to this new audience like never before.

Given the right care and conditions, rugby has a genuine chance to become a true global game of the people, and a real alternative to football or basketball for those who like team sports with a little more bite. The big dream is to consistently deliver F1-meets-Super-Bowl-style moments for a fast-growing, global rugby audience, and this is surely a vision anyone who loves the game can get behind.

It's not often you get an opportunity to build something from scratch. To lean on all the things you've seen over recent years and put them into practice for rugby – the way the NFL, the MLS, the NBA and the UFC all build player fame – is awesome. We have the same big hits, passion, skill, battles and story opportunities – and yet, other than world cups and the Lions, we seldom have those narratives that cut through across your social feed. It's not just about stadium fireworks and social clips – it's about embedding rugby into global culture, making it as much a part of people's weekend routines as Friday night college football, F1 Sundays or the NFL draft event.

There are, and no doubt will continue to be, obstacles put up. The latest whisper is that unions might prevent players from joining. Our belief is that players should have the choice to play wherever they want – enjoying new experiences and challenging themselves to play with and against the best – and, furthermore, unlock whatever commercial opportunities they can for themselves. To help steer us we have assembled a squad of players as well as personalities from the worlds of sport and entertainment – we call them our Game Shapers to, well, help shape the game.

For the players, for the fans, for the game. We have this on our walls in the office. Putting the players first is our commitment. It's what we talk about day in, day out. And as a former player I know all too well that often it's the little things that make the biggest impact – so we're aiming to communicate with them first. Giving them the facts in an adult fashion – not like the teacher–pupil approach that I know happens. From branding and travel ideas to kit and beyond, we want the players to be involved in how we create this game-changing league.

For the players, for the fans, for the game.

25

A SLEEPING GIANT

HASK

Tins is involved in a lot of innovative stuff in rugby. I've known about the breakaway global league that he and a few others are proposing for quite a while, and I really hope they manage to make it work because the sport needs some major disruption.

It will no doubt come down to whether they have enough money or not, because pretty much every scheme that's ever been tried has failed (Rugby X, the brainchild of former England Sevens player and Fiji Sevens coach Ben Ryan, came and went in the blink of an eye a few years back, as did the World 12s, despite the backing of Eddie Jones and former All Blacks head coach Steve Hansen).

I know they've got *some* funding, and there have apparently been multiple bids for franchises from team owners in other sports, but they'll need billions to pull it off. And the current people in charge aren't going to give the game up without a fight.

Since the first *GBR* book, I've worked with business recovery and restructuring firm Leonard Curtis, which was asked to produce a report on rugby. Its findings were very sobering. Not a single Premiership club made a profit in the 2022–23 season, and seven of the clubs were classed as balance sheet insolvent, meaning they were being propped up by their owners. I wrote the foreword to the report, and here is a slightly edited version:

'I think it's fair to say that anyone who knows me, knows that I am not shy in coming forward with my opinions, especially not on the state of our beloved game of rugby union.

'When Leonard Curtis asked me to get involved in this report I said yes quickly. It was a report that was going to finally, unequivocally hold up a mirror to rugby and break through the hyperbole and conjecture to get to the real truth about just where the game is in England.

'It is in my mind a long overdue look that I think paints a bleak picture off the field, even if the product on it is creating some amazing spectacles and huge TV-worthy moments.

'Now I caveat all that with the understanding that I love rugby and a lot of the characters in it. It's a great game that attracts a breed of good people. I don't have an axe to grind but I saw first-hand from the age of 16 to 35 the mistakes being made in the sport, and just how badly things are done in almost every aspect. We say we are professional but in my humble opinion we are far from it and at times resemble the Wild West.

'From what I have seen, experienced and learned, my belief is that the old school values, amateur ethos, and poor business acumen have led to the creation of a top-tier sport in England where in 2022–23 several Premiership clubs could be in financial difficulties.

'It is a sport that has lost three of its teams in a very short period and appears not to have any plan to rectify the damage in the others. Now, Covid-19 didn't help but the overwhelming trend of loss-making was there before the pandemic, and even with the boost of CVC money this has continued and will continue unabated.

'It's clear this is not limited to English clubs. Wales, Scotland, New Zealand and Australia are all facing issues, some more dire than others. There are of course some shining lights, with French TV money growing at a rapid rate, and central contracting in Ireland proving to be the answer to the success of the national team and the regional clubs.

'Rugby for me at the top level is an entertainment business and bears no relation to what happens at grassroots level or what has happened in the past. The fact we have multiple TV deals in the English game and declining ones at that tells you all you need to know about their value and the interest in our game. By comparison, France has one deal that keeps going up. Understanding where and how easily you can view the product itself seems far more difficult than it needs to be.

'There is a great quote by Edward de Bono that always springs to mind when I think about rugby: "*It is historical continuity that maintains most assumptions, not repeated assessment of their validity.*" Rugby appears to believe that just because we have always done it a certain way, that is the right way, when it's clear that unless drastic change happens, our game is heading for a very untenable position in the future.

'The stakeholders need to put their differences aside and unify what they are doing to build a better and sustainable club game in England and frankly globally. The inability to understand who has the power over rugby in England and who runs the game is the first thing that needs addressing.

'We have had several opportunities, especially during Covid, to do what was necessary with the global calendar and restructure the domestic game, but in my view we have again moved at a snail's pace and achieved very little. To my mind, allowing autonomous teams and organisations to do their own thing has not led to success and will not lead to it in the future.

'I had hoped that in reading this report there would be more positives to take from it but I think this is now a line-in-the-sand moment, where all the spin and bravado around how rugby is faring needs to stop and we need to do something drastic.

'Whether that is a franchise model, central contracts, a reduction in teams, stricter monitoring of wage bills, a completely new approach to selling TV rights or something much more severe, we need to change, and change now.

'The passion for this great game is there in both the fans and the players. It is a sport unlike any other. We need to stop trying to be all things to all men and women and own what rugby is, how we can best run it and what will generate income and bums on seats.

'So, I hope this report wakes rugby up. For me, unless the game is run and sold properly it will still be a sleeping giant in years to come.'

We had RFU CEO Bill Sweeney on the podcast, when he was under a lot of pressure to stand down. It had recently been revealed that while the RFU had lost nearly £40 million in reserves, Bill had made £1.1 million, after a £358k bonus was added to his basic salary of £742k. On top of that, Bill was one of six executives who shared a bonus pot of £1.3 million, at a time when the RFU was making more than 40 people redundant. Unsurprisingly, that had caused a lot of resentment in the rugby community and led to the resignation of RFU chairman Tom Ilube.

Bill was quite defiant when we spoke to him, pointing out that the RFU had zero debt, £59 million of cash and £80 million of reserves. But he did admit that the RFU's communication could be poor, and that English rugby had a lot of good stories that weren't being told. I know some newspaper journalists thought we gave him an easy ride, and that his appearance on the podcast helped save his bacon, but it wasn't our fault that he wanted to chat to us and not to them. And we've never claimed to be a hard news outlet.

As far as I'm concerned, Bill's wage is a red herring, because that's just what you'd expect the chief exec of a large business to earn. The real issue is that we have a professional game run with an amateur ethos. Everything about the game at the elite level is undermined by an obsession with grassroots 'values'. The grassroots game and the elite game are two very different things, they just aren't compatible. Don't get me wrong, I've got a lot of time for those grassroots values, but elite rugby should be like any other modern entertainment, full of razzmatazz, big personalities and fast, exciting action.

Bizarrely, rugby sevens – the fastest, most dynamic, potentially most marketable version of the game – is being killed off. The RFU axed England's men's and women's sevens teams in 2020, and the Great Britain's men's and women's full-time programmes were recently scrapped. As well as that, World Rugby has been suffering heavy losses funding the World SVNS Series.

Then there was the Netflix series, *Six Nations: Full Contact*, which was cancelled after just two seasons (actually before the second season had even ended). Formula 1 absolutely nailed it with *Drive to Survive*, the golf documentary *Full Swing* also did pretty well, as did the fly-on-the-wall docs about Wrexham and Sunderland football clubs, but rugby somehow managed to fuck things up.

I've spoken to people in the know, and while Netflix called it *Full Contact* for a reason, because they expected that no access would be denied, teams apparently fought them on everything. Certain players, coaches and backroom staff didn't want to talk, and teams denied camera crews access to certain areas, including changing rooms.

The teams' bigwigs needed to be saying, 'I don't care if you don't want cameras in the changing room at half-time, cameras are going into the changing room at half-time. And if a coach calls a couple of his players wankers and throws a cup of coffee at them, we're going to put that in, because that's the reality, and that's what viewers want to see.' All the other docs I've mentioned had those controversies, but rugby wasn't interested in creating those moments and promoting personalities, so no wonder Netflix binned it.

All of the above is why somebody needed to step in, and why Tins and his mates have done that. The plan is for all the sport's best talent to play for franchises in a travelling carnival, like F1 weekends, in some of the best cities in the world. They've designed the calendar so that it won't interfere with international rugby, because not allowing those guys to play for their countries would not be good for the sport.

If it comes off, hopefully the Premiership will reset with an influx of younger talent and reduced salary caps, which might make the clubs sustainable as businesses. It's not about stopping players earning good money, it's about accepting that there isn't the money available. But if franchises can take the best players out of the Premiership and pay them top dollar, maybe Premiership clubs can consolidate, and those younger players will be on better money than they otherwise would have been.

Tins doesn't want to kill English rugby, he wants to save it, and his proposed R360 competition reminds me of Kerry Packer's World Series Cricket in the late 1970s, when the Aussie media tycoon signed up many of the world's best players, who were being paid peanuts by their cricket boards, and had them playing 'Supertests' all over Australia, New Zealand and the West Indies. It was a good standard of cricket and the players were paid well.

World Series Cricket only last a couple of years, but it changed the game in many ways. As reviled as Packer was at the time, he essentially invented modern cricket: floodlit matches, coloured clothing, helmets, franchises, merchandising, big broadcast deals, the world's best players getting paid their dues.

Packer's most enduring legacy was the lesson that cricket was a marketable game that could generate huge revenues, rather than a gentle pastime that always seemed to be rooted in the past.

Rugby's authorities now, like cricket's authorities back then, seem to think they're untouchable. But while tradition is lovely, it can't be the driver of any professional sport. Traditions can become like millstones, and they sometimes need to be cut free so that a sport can move forward. That happened in cricket, and it will happen in rugby. It's just a matter of when.

THE THANK YOUS

First, thank you, dear reader, for buying this! We said it at the start, but we are nothing without the listeners, fans and followers of everything we do. We are continuously amazed by what this pod has become – and every time someone says hello, asks for a picture or apologises for being a nause we're grateful, and surprised. Even if Hask plays it cool.

Thank you to Nic, our long-suffering MD of the last five years, who has put out more fires, saved more events, salvaged more travel plans, ordered more cups of coffee, chased more invoices and calmed more HR issues, court cases and tribunals than any man should ever have to. He is, wisely, off to a new challenge in the world of health and wellness. We can't possibly think why.

Thank you to all the team behind GBR and Good, Bad, Media. We're not easy, we don't listen, we can't concentrate, we're never on time, we're rarely facing the right way, Tins is never off his phone and Hask is … fill in the blank. Payno's pretty good. And picks up the scraps. Like this. Hopefully, in among the chaos, it's a lot of fun.

Thank you to the team at HarperCollins – especially Ajda, who is definitely going to be signing up for one of Nic's new courses after working through her second book with us. Apologies for all the WhatsApp messages, late-night calls, scraps of script, unfinished chapters, last-minute panics and general apathy in the face of your rigid deadlines. This wouldn't have got anywhere near the shelves without your powers of persuasion and brilliant editing. Also, thank you to Ben Dirs for his help and patience writing the book with us.

Finally, thank you to all the coaches, teachers, executive producers, agents and therapists who went into getting the three of us to this point. You're all responsible in some way or other for this mess. And we couldn't thank you more.

Thanks, Dream Team. And onwards.